Write and C
for Deeper Learning

28 evidence-based and easy-to-apply tactics
that will make your instruction better for learning

Patti Shank, PhD

Make It Learnable Series

v2.5.2017

Quantity discounts:
This book is available in print and electronic formats on Amazon and from pattishank.com. To obtain quantity discounts for your work team, class, or workshop, contact Patti: patti@pattishank.com.

Patti Shank PhD/Learning Peaks LLC
Learning sPeaks Publications
www.pattishank.com

Write and Organize for Deeper Learning/ Patti Shank PhD —1st ed, update 1.
ISBN-13: 978-1545162408
ISBN-10: 1545162409

Praise for *Write and Organize for Deeper Learning*

Don't you love it when a master demonstrates her knowledge and expertise? Well, Patti Shank does just that with her latest book on designing instructional materials. You can view every one of the 28 evidence-based tactics presented in her book in action—right before your eyes! This is the most practical how-to-write book on the market.
***Elaine Biech, Author of* The Business of Consulting *and* The Art and Science of Training**

Write and Organize for Deeper Learning is a treasure trove of high-value, on-target, evidence-based guidance. The book is packed with practical, straight-forward techniques for making your instructional prose effective, efficient and impactful. I strongly recommend this book for anyone who has to write instructional scripts, content, storyboards, job aids, or any instructional material, online or off.
Karl Kapp, Ed.D., Professor, Instructional Technology, Bloomsburg University, and author of "The Gamification of Learning and Instruction."

As a career trainer and instructional designer, I found Patti Shank's *Write and Organize for Deeper Learning* fascinating! I've cobbled my knowledge of good design from years of experience and believed I was doing the best I could. I was wrong! The strategies and tactics here did two things: confirmed what I thought was right, so I can keep doing it, and helped me correct and improve. I recommend Patti Shank's *Write and Organize for Deeper Learning* for instructional writers, trainers and anyone who wants to teach for understanding and retention. My writing is already clearer.
Karen Hyder, Online Event Producer and Speaker Coach, GuildMaster 2017, KarenHyder.com

Patti Shank's book on "writing for learning" hits the bull's eye with its lucidity and practical ideas. I love the way she has provided a scientific reasoning for why we should follow her recommended strategies. That makes a lot of sense and adds to the "learnability" of this book. Thanks, Patti, for this short and useful handbook for instructional writers.
Madhavi Sardeshpande, Learning Strategist, Accenture's Global Talent Research Team

When I was notified *Write and Organize for Deeper Learning* was available, I was skeptical. Most of the books in the profession dip into the absurdities and myths of learning. But, when I saw it was from Patti, my first instinct was to give it a quick skim. My skimming became a thorough reading, and I am glad it did. Patti has created a gem of a book, in a treasure trove of a series. This is the first book, and she already has me looking forward to the others. Get it! Read it! Buy copies for people who ask you how to become trainers or instructional designers! Or give it to the training department within your own organization! If any training professional reads this and puts these scientifically-supported tactics into practice, they will help their organization produce better training outcomes. They will become better trainers. And they will have learners thanking them for producing an outstanding course.
Bill Sawyer, Director, Global Learning Services, Seal Software

This work wouldn't have happened without the support of two important people. With deep gratitude to Brent and Jessica. You are my personal superheroes.

Thank to Bill Sawyer for his help in making this book better. When a reader is willing to help you (a lot), it's a rare gift.

Thanks to the Association for Talent Development (ATD), whose desire to offer this kind of content helped me move forward.

Table of Contents

CHAPTER 1

Introduction

In this part of the book, I tell you why I wrote the book, explain why writing for instruction is different from other types of writing, and discuss how to use the book. It's short and sweet. Like me.

Helping People Learn

The Make It Learnable series applies key learning, writing, and information design principles to remove needless obstacles to learning and help people learn, apply, and retain needed information.

Many people who write instructional content have an inaccurate picture of how adults learn. Learning is more complex than most people realize. Without an accurate understanding, it is difficult to build the best instructional content. The learning sciences are complicated, but the good news is that applying them isn't. The intention of this series is to offer information about what the learning sciences are and, more importantly, how to apply them.

Research shows that work increasingly requires difficult mental tasks and frequent updating and addition of skills. Our ability to help people learn these tasks and add skills is one of the critical keys to supporting work. That's why this book, like others in the series, aims precisely at helping make instructional content better for learning.

We need all kinds of people to teach others in this world. The more capable and skilled people we have in the world, the better the world is for everyone. I discuss building adult instructional content in organizational learning settings, but you should be able to apply it to other adult learning settings as well.

After a brief introduction, I offer an overview of the science (research) that supports the four strategies and 28 tactics described in the book. I wrote it in mostly non-academic language (but I use some academic terms because they are extremely helpful) to help you understand why we need the strategies and tactics in the rest of the book.

I then discuss key learning, writing, and information design tactics you should use to make your content more learnable and better for today's organizational learning conditions.

I assume you already know the basics of writing. If you need help in this area, please find a writing coach. Even if you write well, it is quite helpful to work with an editor. I use an editor with all my books and larger works. I remember how upset my mom was that I struggled with tense and spelling when I was in school. Yep, I *need* an editor. Still.

My goal is to help you make your ideas better *for instruction*. Thanks for taking this journey with me.

Writing for Instruction

Because of its intent, writing for instruction differs from other kinds of writing. People who write for instruction write for a specific purpose: *learnability*. Learnability describes how easily content may be learned, applied, and remembered.

Consider the example learning topics below. For each topic, think of one thing a person should be able to do after they take part in training on that topic. Table 1.1 lists something a participant should be able to do after taking part in training on each topic.

Learning topics:

- Protect Your PC from Viruses and Malware
- Financial Statements: Profit & Loss (P&L)
- Employment Law 101
- Apache Spark Libraries

Table 1.1 Learning topics and something a person should be able to do

Learning topic	**What should a person be able to *do*?**
Protect Your PC from Viruses and Malware	Take specific steps to reduce the chances of infecting a computer with malicious software.
Financial Statements: Profit & Loss (P&L)	Analyze the profitability of a department or company using its P&L statement.
Employment Law 101	Analyze what managers can and cannot do when hiring, firing, and managing people.
Apache Spark Libraries	Use Apache Spark's built-in libraries, including SQL queries, streaming data, machine learning, and graph processing, while working with large datasets.

Because our goal is to help people learn to *do* something, we certainly don't want what we write or how we present the instruction to get in the way of building these skills. Instructional writing means building instructional content (text, graphics, video, audio, etc.) with the primary purpose *of helping people learn, apply, and remember.*

Are you an instructional writer? You are if you are an expert who teaches others what you know and do; a faculty member or instructor; or a teacher, trainer, or instructional designer who builds instructional content.

Most instruction builds from text: prose, a script, description, steps in a process, and so on. There are ways to write that foster learning. As an instructional writer, you do not need to write novels or other creative works of art. Your job is to write in a way that helps your audience learn, apply, and remember what you write.

Other writers may get away with writing and leaving it up to their readers to try to understand. But instructional writers cannot do this, as they must make their content easy to understand *and* easy to use. So, instructional writing usually requires writers to go through at least two stages:

1. **Draft** from a writer's (or an expert's) perspective. (Better still, if you're more experienced, draft from the user's perspective.)
2. **Revise** from a user's perspective. (And revise again to answer users' questions and make the information they need easy to find. And, if possible, have prospective users offer comments from which to revise again.)

My recommendations are consistent with the principles of good writing. For example, your high school teacher may have told you to avoid the passive voice. It's generally better to write *The owners met the deadline to correct the safety violations* (active) than *The deadline to correct the safety violations was met by the owners* (passive).

But I base these recommendations on learnability rather than on style considerations. Sentences written in active voice are typically shorter and clearer than sentences that express the same idea in passive voice. Writing concisely and clearly helps reduce the amount of mental processing needed during reading.

People who write for instruction are different from other types of writers. They make decisions based on what will best help their audience learn, apply, and remember.

Using This Book

This book tackles four specific strategies. For each strategy, I discuss specific actionable tactics you can implement this very moment. For each tactic, I show examples and discuss issues. Here are the four strategies we will discuss.

Strategy 1: Understand your audience's needs.

Strategy 2: Write for clarity.

Strategy 3: Make text readable and legible.

Strategy 4: Organize for memory and use.

How to improve your skills using this book

Throughout this book, I suggest ways to practice the skills listed. But don't feel you need to wait for me! There are two excellent ways to strengthen your understanding, and I suggest doing both.

- **Summarize** each section in your own words. Research shows that "self-explanations" are a powerful method for increasing understanding. This simply means summarizing in your own words, which helps build a model of the topic in your own mind (we call this *building schemas*). Use this instructional method in your own courses, too!
- **Apply** each section to your own content. If you know of others who are using this book, share how you apply the tactics. Offer feedback to each other.

When should you use these strategies and tactics?

This book applies to textual learning content, such as readings, descriptions, and words on screens or slides. It also applies to text you write for audio and video scripts. Since almost all instructional content begins as text, it applies almost universally. In stories and scenarios, realistic dialogue may take priority over some of these methods.

In the next chapter, "The Science," I begin by discussing the learning science that supports the strategies and tactics discussed in the rest of the chapters. Understanding the science helps you understand the choice of strategies and tactics in the rest of the book. For example, why can't we teach lots and lots of content at a time? And what is so important about learnability?

I love this content because research shows that it makes a real difference in learning outcomes. If you have suggestions for improving it, I want to hear from you. I am self-publishing the Make It Learnable series, so I can easily maintain and update it. You can get in touch with me through the contact form on my website (www.pattishank.com) if you have comments to make it better.

CHAPTER 2

The Science

This part of the book explores the core research that helps us understand what we need to do to help people learn, apply, and remember instruction. It explains the whys behind the how-tos in Chapters 3, 4, 5, and 6. You could skip this. But please don't.

People who cook and do home improvement work may not know the science behind what they do; but, if they are good at the tasks involved, they *apply* the science used in their field. When people who bake don't apply chemistry, recipes fail. When people who build walls don't apply physics and mathematics, their walls aren't straight and don't stay standing. They don't need to understand the science, but they apply it or their work doesn't work.

Too many people who design instruction don't realize that this is true for instruction, too. People have long found ways to learn in not-very-good situations, so many people think there isn't any science. But there's just as much science in helping people learn as there is in building walls and baking cakes. In today's super-busy workplaces, where people need to learn continually, it's irresponsible not to apply these tactics that make learning easier and deeper.

You've no doubt been the recipient of instruction that didn't apply the science. You've likely been in instructional settings where the instructor had to "get through a lot of content." They kept going even after your mind couldn't take any more. You've probably experienced what people called training that was nothing more than someone talking at you, without any practice.

In this section, I start with a discussion of some of the major areas of research that tell us how people learn best. You *could* skip this chapter and go right to the how-to sections, which start in Chapter 3. But, if you want to know why the strategies and tactics work, start here.

I try to stay away from academic jargon, but it does help to know a few of the terms. In this section, I talk about seven critical areas of research that improve learnability: readability, usability, memory, prior knowledge, mental effort, deep learning, and metacognition (Figure 2.1).

Figure 2.1 Seven areas that can improve learnability

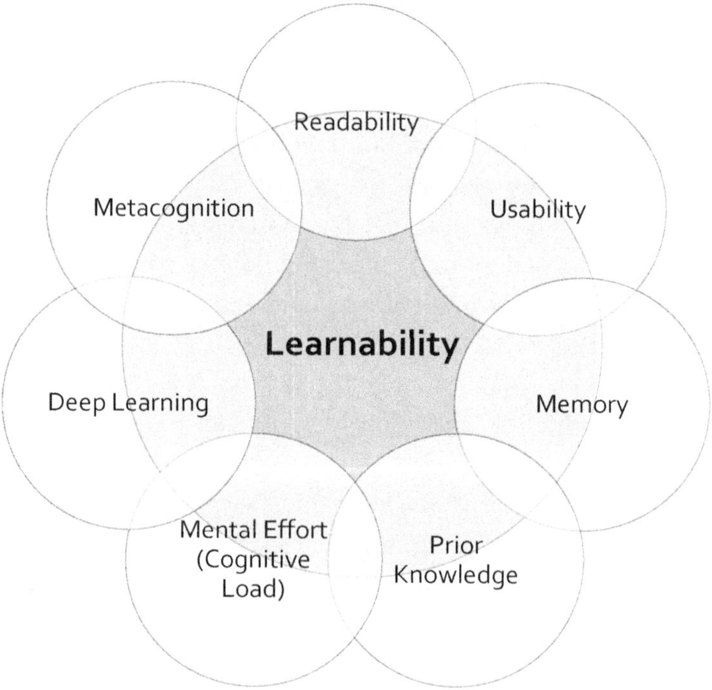

Insights and outcomes from these research areas help us understand how to make learning work better for people in today's fast-changing work environments. The examples in the following sections come primarily from adult and organizational learning. If you work in other areas of learning, you should not find it difficult to make connections to those areas as well.

Learnability

Learnability is the ease and speed with which something can be learned, applied, and remembered.

Learnability applied to a new type of window means that people can figure out and remember how to use it. Learnability applied to a new smartphone means people can easily learn how to do the things they want and need to do (make calls, import contacts, change settings, and so forth). Learnability applied to organizational learning means people can easily use instruction, performance support, and other tools to get work done and improve skills (complete tasks, fix problems, and so on).

Maria Costabile, a professor at the University of Bari, Italy, where she teaches human-computer interaction, and her fellow authors discuss the need to make e-learning easier to use in their article on usability in e-learning. They say we risk making learning and work harder because we do not understand how to create synergies between what we build and what people need. This is my reason for writing the Make It Learnable series.

Two concepts help us understand learnability: readability and usability. Both are critical to the design of instructional materials.

Readability

Readability is the ease with which a text can be read and understood. A readability formula calculates text metrics for a given reading passage, using syllable count, sentence length, and word difficulty. It then returns a score that reflects the complexity of the measured text. Different formulas for computing readability, however, may focus on slightly different aspects of writing.

John Guthrie, a scholar and researcher in literacy studies, found that readability is a good stand-in for complex learnability formulas. That means that we can use readability formulas to approximate whether what we've written is learnable. This makes logical sense. If something isn't easily readable, it won't be easy to learn from it.

Rudolf Flesch devised Flesch Reading Ease (Table 2.1), which we see in the readability calculations in Microsoft Word. (In Chapter 5, I discuss how you can perform this calculation.)

Table 2.1 Flesch Reading Ease Scores

Score	**Description**
100-90	Easy to read. U.S. 5th-grade level.
80-90	Easy to read. U.S. 6th-grade level.
70-80	Fairly easy to read. U.S. 7th-grade level.
60-70	Plain language. U.S. 8th- to 9th-grade level.
50-60	Somewhat difficult to read. U.S. 10th- to 11th-grade level.
30-50	Difficult to read. College-level reading.

Shawn Badgley, Communications and Digital Outreach Manager at The Rhode Island Historical Society, Syracuse University, tells us that an 8th-grade reading level is right for most readers. He comments that even *Harvard Business Review* writes at this level on much of its website. They simply want to get their ideas across to the largest possible audience.

To decide whether you should write in this sweet spot or cater to a niche audience, consider building personas for your audience. Personas are made-up people captured from the characteristics of the primary people you are building content for. Personas help us know the needs we most need to meet. You don't need a persona for every possible audience type. Just the ones you most need to meet.

For example, one of the personas I built for this series of books is a veterinarian who writes practice management books and builds instructional workshops. This helps me make sure these books make sense to a variety of experts who very much want to meet the needs of their participants but who are not likely to understand all the academic jargon. And that's fine, because they don't need to.

I wrote this book using Microsoft Word and checked the readability using Flesch Reading Ease. It scored 60.6. I intentionally included examples of poor learnability in this book, and those bad examples are included in that score. I edited and rewrote sections of the book that were more difficult to read, because I wrote this book for anyone who writes instruction and wants to make it better for learning.

Question: What do you think? Does intentionally writing at an 8th- or 9th-grade level dumb down the content? (Try to not look at the answer until you have formed your own answer.)

Answer: We may choose to write instructional content at an 8th- or 9th-grade level to make text faster and easier to process. This is because people must read a lot of content at work and elsewhere.

We too often assume that people will be able to understand what we write because we understand it. For example, research on home pregnancy test instructions in the early 1980s found them to have unfamiliar and technical terms that could reduce the clarity of the directions. The authors of the study suggested revising the instructions for easier reading and application.

Workers have a lot to read and understand. Most don't have the time, bandwidth, or energy to figure out what something means. Instruction must be learnable to be valuable. Learnability starts with readability.

Usability

The Usability Body of Knowledge (www.usabilitybok.org), a regularly updated resource developed by the User Experience Professionals Association, says that usability is "the degree to which something—software, hardware, or anything else—is easy to use and a good fit for the people who use it." Usability considers learnability one of the most important of all usability goals.

Usability professionals' principles largely come from the science of perception and memory. They work to make human work easier by making human-made systems easier. Doing so can improve the outcomes of work.

People who design instruction *also* need to use the science of perception and memory (and other sciences) to improve human work. Costabile and fellow authors explain that, when our materials are less learnable, people must spend time and mental effort figuring out how to use them and get beyond the distractions and other difficulties that divert learning. When people must do this, they have less time and mental effort for learning (Figure 2.2).

Figure 2.2 Good instruction reduces distractions and wasted mental effort to allow more mental effort for learning.

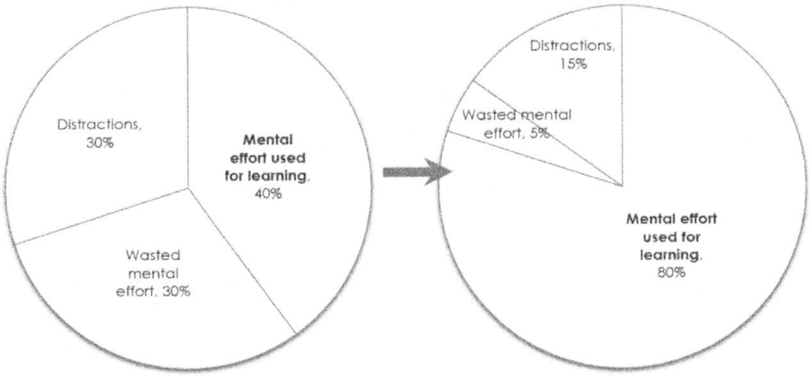

Good usability means we avoid unnecessary distractions and problems that divert learning. What they know, and what you should know, is that the need to avoid distractions and other difficulties in learning comes primarily from wasted memory and mental effort, which I discuss in the next two sections. I selected many of the strategies and tactics in this book because they reduce the distractions and wasted mental effort that make it harder to learn.

Using the tactics in this book will make your materials more learnable. Learnable materials are easier to learn, apply, and remember.

The following are two of the most important implications of learnability for instruction.

- ✓ Learnability requires that we understand what the audience needs and use evidence-based practice.
- ✓ Don't stop at readability measures. But readability is a good starting point for more learnable materials.

Try It

How would you explain learnability in your own words? How does learnability apply to the instruction you build? Go to page 26 and explain learnability and how it applies to the instruction you build. Don't skip this! It will help you understand and remember this concept!

Prior Knowledge

John Bransford, who was a Professor of Education at University of Washington College of Education and a critical contributor to the science of learning, helps us understand that what people already know is the foundation for adding more knowledge. When we learn, the new information alters what already we know.

This is how we make sense of new information. We mix new information into existing schemas (schemas are how we think our mind organizes information and how information is related to other information) or we begin new schemas, which get refined as we learn more. It is our job to help people build accurate schemas.

For example, when learning how to make sauces, those who have made a sauce that uses a roux (pronounced *roo*), which is made by cooking flour and fat together and then adding liquid, will find that making any other roux-based sauce is similar. This includes sauces like béchamel, velouté, Creole, bordelaise, Périgueux, and Mornay.

But what happens when people have no prior knowledge of roux-based sauces? Then we'll want to help them understand how something familiar is similar so they understand the concept. Perhaps they have added hot water to instant oatmeal. If they add the water too fast, they'll end up with clumps of oatmeal and hot water. So, they must add the hot water slowly, incorporating it gradually into the oatmeal. The same principle applies when adding hot liquids into the roux.

Adults come to us with a great deal of prior knowledge. Working with what they already know helps makes content learnable.

The following are a few of the most important implications of prior knowledge for instruction.

- ✓ Don't assume people have a certain amount of prior knowledge.
- ✓ Connect what you are teaching to what people already know to help new information stick.
- ✓ Find and fix misunderstandings. Building new knowledge on a faulty foundation creates even more misunderstandings.
- ✓ Don't teach people with diverse levels of knowledge similarly. They have different needs and require different learning strategies.

Try It

How would you explain prior knowledge in your own words? How does prior knowledge apply to the instruction you build? Go to page 26 and explain prior knowledge and how it applies to the instruction you build. Don't skip this! It will help you understand and remember this concept!

Memory

John Sweller, a well-known educational psychologist and researcher, explains that we must design for *human cognitive architecture* so people can learn. That sounds like complicated gobbledygook, but it mostly means we must design for how our mind and memory works. Figure 2.3 shows the basic memory processes happening during learning.

Figure 2.3 Learning processes involving memory (from Elsbeth Stern and Lennart Schalk, Source: https://www.nature.com/articles/s41539-016-0003-0#Sec6, used with permission)

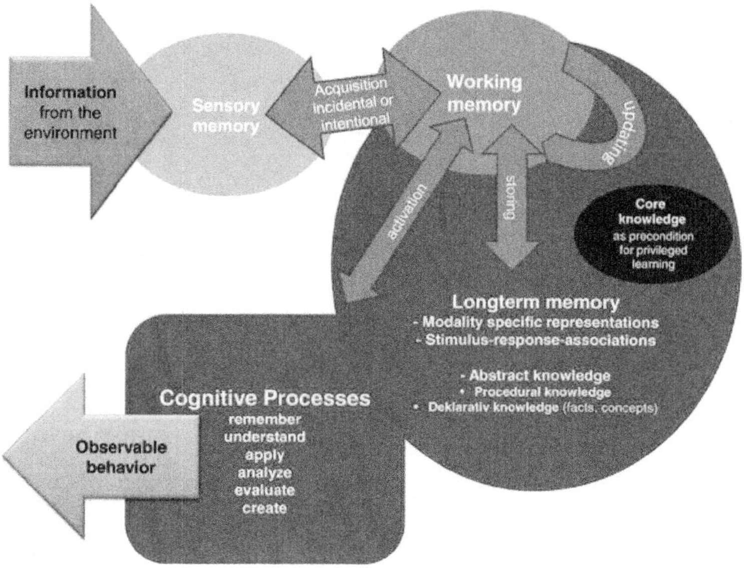

Our senses take in information from our environment. Working memory (WM) filters out irrelevant and non-useful information and selects essential elements. for processing. This filtering occurs because our senses are continuously bombarded with information (sounds, images, and so on).

Since WM can process only a few things at a time, it must select from incoming information and use prior knowledge (in schemas) from long-term memory to decide what's important. When processing information, WM also retrieves information from long-term memory (LTM) to put new information in context (make sense of it). It also determines how the new information should be stored (in schemas) in LTM.

WM is a limited resource. It has limited capacity (the amount it can process) and limited time (how long it is held). Unless transferred to LTM, incoming information is lost. The information that makes it to LTM alters prior knowledge by adding to it and is transformed by prior knowledge by giving it context.

The following are a few of the most important implications of memory for instruction.

- ✓ Eliminate unnecessary content and distractions so WM isn't overloaded.
- ✓ Write and organize to make it easier to see what is important.
- ✓ Help others who build or approve instructional materials understand why building for memory constraints is critical.

Working memory has very limited capacity, and it is in heavy demand during work and learning. One of our main responsibilities when designing learning is to reduce unnecessary demands on WM.

Questions: Look at Figure 2.3 and see if you can answer the following questions. (Try to not look at my answers until you have formed your own answers.)

1. How is WM used in instruction?

2. How is LTM used in instruction?

Answers:

1. How is WM used in instruction?

WM is the active part of memory, and we use it whenever we learn something new or retrieve information from LTM. Because we are literally bombarded with stimuli, we must design instruction to help people pay attention to the most important things.

2. How is LTM used in instruction?

If you pondered these questions before looking at the answers, you used LTM to figure out what you already knew (prior knowledge) and brought it to WM. LTM and WM are very active players in learning! Because WM can hold only a short amount of information for a brief time, we must design instruction to not overwhelm WM.

Try It

How would you explain memory (WM and LTM) in your own words? How do these different kinds of memory apply to the instruction you build? Go to page 26 and explain memory and how it applies to the instruction you build. Don't skip this! It will help you understand and remember this concept!

Mental Effort (Cognitive Load)

When we design for learnability and understand that working memory (WM) needs to process all new information but has considerable constraints (in capacity for new material and holding time), we realize WM is one of the most important constraints we must deal with when designing instruction. (Accurate and adequate prior knowledge, on the other hand, *helps* people learn.)

A person I once worked with told me her training group had to train people on large quantities of information very quickly. "It's like drinking out of a firehose," she said, and she asked how they could do it better. My response was a bit too abrupt, but it's true nonetheless: Anyone who must drink out of a firehose will die of thirst, because you cannot drink out of a firehose.

Sweller reminds us we must design *with* how memory works; otherwise, people don't learn. His research shows us that cognitive load is the amount of mental effort needed to process current information. Working memory—the part of memory we use to process information in the present moment—can deal with only so much content at a time. Too much information overloads working memory.

We learn most effectively by comparing knowledge in working memory to knowledge in long-term memory (prior knowledge). A working memory clogged with too much content cannot do this. Our ability to make sense of what we hear is impaired when there is too much noise. Our ability to learn is impaired when there is too much to learn at once.

Not all cognitive load is the same. Some is helpful; some is harmful. We call the harmful type *extraneous* cognitive load and, when we don't design instruction well, we can cause it.

Here are some examples of extraneous (harmful) cognitive load:

- Extra content that isn't on target or that isn't needed now
- Non-valuable or decorative graphics
- Unnecessary explanations
- Explanations that are not nearby what they explain
- Media that doesn't allow stopping, starting, and rewinding

Question: What have I already discussed that would explain why these examples of extraneous cognitive load are harmful? (Try to not look at my answers until you have formed your own answers.)

Answer: They all use a very limited resource: working memory. Since they do not help learning and they use a valuable resource, they interfere with learning. You now know one of the most critical tips for designing instruction: Save working memory for important tasks.

You may be wondering what *helpful* cognitive load is. The mental effort needed to learn is helpful cognitive load. It's helpful because it's necessary—unlike harmful cognitive load, which is unnecessary. The following are some examples of helpful cognitive load.

- Doing self-check exercises
- Comparing your wrong answers to the right answers
- Framing a question to be sure you understand
- Putting what you read into your own words
- Practicing tasks until they are easy to do

This is a good time to clarify that not all helpful cognitive load is fun. "Necessary to learning" and "fun" are two different things. Part of learning—especially when learning harder things—is making it through the hard parts until they become easier. You know this if you've learned to play an instrument. Or a sport. A former Navy Seal in one of my training classes said, "You do it over and over until you can do it effortlessly. This helps you come back alive from missions." Most of us have never been in that kind of situation, but the point remains—learning can be effortful and difficult. Can you think of things you have struggled to learn?

The following are two of the most important implications of cognitive load for instruction.

- ✓ Build instruction that supports helpful cognitive load and eliminates bad cognitive load.
- ✓ Help others who build or approve instructional materials understand why eliminating bad cognitive load is critical.

Supporting good cognitive load and eliminating bad cognitive load makes content more learnable. This is one of the most important things we can do to support learning.

Try It

How would you explain cognitive load in your own words? How does cognitive load apply to the instruction you build? Go to page 26 and explain cognitive load and how it applies to the instruction you build. Don't skip this! It will help you understand and remember this concept!

Deep Learning

Until the 1970s, the issue of "depth" of learning wasn't discussed or researched. Two professors at the University of Gothenburg, Ference Marton and Roger Säljö, did groundbreaking research on the depth of mental (cognitive) processing while learning, which began a continuing conversation about (and research into) what they called surface and deep learning approaches and their outcomes.

Marton and Säljö asked students to read an article and answer questions about it. They transcribed the conversations and analyzed them, finding two different approaches to reading and interpreting the article: surface and deep. A surface approach focused on the main points. A deep approach looked for the meaning behind these points and how they related to each other and other knowledge.

Surface learning is not *bad*. But it is usually not enough for applied skills. Deeper learning is needed to gain and maintain usable skills. This book concentrates on deep learning approaches using relevant and meaningful learning tasks and strategies. You don't have to know what those are just yet. I'll explain them simply and with a lot of examples.

The following are a few of the most important implications of deep learning for instruction.

- ✓ We need to help people learn deeply, both in formal instruction and on their own, as jobs are becoming less routine and more complex.
- ✓ Deep learning approaches support application and usable skills.

Deep learning supports skill building and it is our ultimate destination for job-related learning. Making instruction learnable helps people understand, remember, and apply.

How would you explain deep learning in your own words? How does deep learning apply to the instruction you build? Go to page 26 and explain learnability and how it applies to the instruction you build. Don't skip this! It will help you understand and remember this concept!

Metacognition

Metacognition is an awareness of one's own thinking and learning processes. (*Cognition* means thinking, so metacognition means thinking about your thinking.) It's one of the most important learning and life skills because it makes us better and more self-sufficient learners and workers. John Flavell, a developmental psychologist, coined the term "metacognition" to reference how we think about our thinking.

Metacognitive processes allow us to use prior knowledge to plan how to approach a given learning task, monitor our progress, solve problems, evaluate how we are doing, and change our approach as needed. These skills help us apply what we know about ourselves, what we know about different strategies for learning, and what we know about the demands of a specific learning task. Flavell divided metacognitive strategies into three categories:

- Personal: What people know about themselves, such as that they feel most secure in doing a task after they have practiced it successfully many times.
- Strategy: The strategies people know how to use, such as making an outline, writing a list of questions, and getting those questions answered.
- Task: What people know or can find out about a task and what they need to do to perform it, such as getting insights from others who have successfully performed it about the best ways to learn it so the skills "stick."

It is critical to learn throughout our work life so, as designers and facilitators of learning, we should embed these three categories of metacognitive strategies in our instruction. Research clearly shows that using metacognitive strategies during instruction helps people learn to apply them elsewhere in their lives.

Plan learning goals

Before instruction:

- Look at the content and activities to decide whether they are at the right level for the participants.
- Identify the outcomes that are most important to the participants.
- Figure out what efforts the participants need to successfully achieve the desired results.
- Decide what help the participants will likely need.
- Identify what has worked for the participants in learning similar things before.
- Figure out what the participants already know about this task or group of tasks.
- Uncover misconceptions that can mess up the participants' learning.

Monitor progress

During instruction, we can:

- Identify what participants do and do not understand.
- Summarize the key points in the participants' own words (this helps build schemas).
- Find added resources for personal areas of interest not covered in instruction.
- Use "help" that was identified during planning to work on areas of weakness.
- Develop questions.
- Compare questions to see who can answer them.
- Decide what still feels too hard and what participants need to do.
- Look for areas of wide confusion (so an instructor or subject-matter expert can adjust instruction).
- Share what participants are going to implement.

Evaluate strategies and outcomes

During and after instruction, we can help participants:

- Reflect on the learning experience.
- Determine which strategies worked well for them.
- Review initial planning steps and decide whether any changes are needed.
- Develop strategies for learning and applying this content.
- Support themselves in learning and applying the content.
- Check in with themselves on what is working or not working in their application of the strategies.

Metacognitive strategies are life-long learning skills. One of the ways we prepare people for the realities of rapidly changing job skills is by using these strategies in our instruction.

> The following are two of the most important implications of metacognition for instruction.
>
> ✓ Use metacognitive strategies yourself when learning how to develop effective instruction.
>
> ✓ Use metacognitive strategies in instruction to help people become effective life-long learners.

More and more, people must learn on their own as skills change and morph on the job. Learnable resources and materials make it easier for people to become self-sufficient learners.

Try It

How would you explain metacognition in your own words? How does metacognition apply to the instruction you build? Go to page 26 and explain metacognition and how it applies to the instruction you build. Don't skip this! It will help you understand and remember this concept!

In Your Own Words

Self-explanations are a powerful tool to help you integrate new and prior knowledge. They involve describing what you learned in your own words.

For each of the concepts in this chapter, explain them in your own words, including how each concept applies to your instructional materials.

Learnability

Memory

Prior Knowledge

Mental Effort (Cognitive Load)

Deep Learning

Metacognition

CHAPTER 3

Strategy 1: Understand Your Audience's Needs

Chapter 2 discussed the underlying research (the WHY) that helps us understand the need for the rest of the book (the HOW). In this chapter and the following three chapters, I describe four strategies and 28 tactics you should use when you write and organize instructional content (Table 3.1).

You may want to bookmark Table 3.1 for ease of finding in the future. It shows the organization of the strategies and tactics. Referring back to this table may help you organize the material in your mind.

Table 3.1 Writing and organizing strategies and tactics

Chapter 3	Strategy 1: Understand your audience's needs	Tactic 1: Analyze Your Audience's Needs Tactic 2: Write for the Right Level of Prior Knowledge Tactic 3: Make the Purpose Obvious Tactic 4: Answer Audience Questions
Chapter 4	Strategy 2: Write for clarity	Tactic 5: Determine Your Key Points Tactic 6: Use Shorter Sentences Tactic 7: Remove Less Valuable Sentences Tactic 8: Use Simpler, More Common Words and Phrases Tactic 9: Talk Directly to Your Reader/Listener Tactic 10: Prefer Active Voice Tactic 11: Be Direct about What People Need to Do Tactic 12: Make Long Descriptions Easier to Understand
Chapter 5	Strategy 3: Make text readable and legible	Tactic 13: Test Readability Tactic 14: Use Readable Fonts Tactic 15: Use Readable Type Sizes Tactic 16: Left-align Body Text Tactic 17: Use Adequate White Space Tactic 18: Space Lines of Text for Ease of Reading Tactic 19: Use Readable Line Lengths Tactic 20: Offer Adequate Contrast between Text and Background
Chapter 6	Strategy 4: Organize for memory and use	Tactic 21: Connect to What People Already Know Tactic 22: Design for Scanning Tactic 23: Write Clear, Reader-friendly Objectives Tactic 24: Tell People Where They Are Going Tactic 25: Use Signals Tactic 26: Make Content Job-ready Tactic 27: Write Helpful Headings and Sub-headings Tactic 28: Move Less-essential Content to Non-prime Space

Many people who develop instruction start with writing what they know—or taking what a subject-matter expert knows—and putting it into authoring tools. NOT okay! Understanding our audience must come first as it helps us know what they need to be able to learn, apply, and remember.

If we don't understand our audience or their jobs, building good instruction is practically impossible to do. This is because helping people do a good job and increase skills is a critical goal for organizational learning. We must tailor content to the need or it will not be useful.

Information bombards us every day: mail, email, text messages, social media, information coming home with our children from school, ads, television, content that people want us to look at. Our brain is exploding with things to take in. But you learned earlier that we simply cannot attend to all of this. Our minds must be selectively attentive. If your instructional message isn't equally selective, your message may not get through.

For example, many people in a hospital setting encounter medical waste—and medical waste products such as blood and body tissues can be hazardous. But the settings and situations in which medical staff, non-medical staff, and patients and their families encounter medical waste are different.

Different people have different prior knowledge, and they don't all understand the same things. The wording of instructional content for medical and nursing staff will be different than that for transport staff or family. People who go to different parts of the hospital may encounter different types of medical waste and may need to take different types of precautions. As you learned in the previous chapter, we cannot simply tell everyone *everything* they might ever need to know. Overwhelming people with information is similar to telling them nothing.

In Strategy 1, we discuss four tactics you can use to understand your audience's needs and to tailor your instruction (Figure 3.1).

Figure 3.1 Tactics that help us learn about and write for our audience's needs

Tactic 1: Analyze Your Audience's Needs
Tactic 2: Write for the Right Level of Prior Knowledge
Tactic 3: Make the Purpose Obvious
Tactic 4: Answer Audience Questions

Tactic 1: Analyze Your Audience's Needs

When we design instruction, we need to understand our audience's lives or work so that what we develop meets their needs. If we don't perform this critical task, our ability to support them will be hit-or-miss. This is especially true today, when people are constantly learning new information and tasks. Table 3.1 shows typical ways to understand the work that people do.

Table 3.1 Ways to understand your audience's work

Method	Description
1. Watch general work and specific tasks.	Watch people work to see what they do and how they do it. Watch specific tasks for which you are designing training. Make sure you don't bias answers with your own thoughts or feelings.
2. Ask questions.	Ask questions about the work and specific tasks. Show training plans and materials to get feedback. Ask unbiased questions to get the same information from various people. Ask more questions based on what people say. Don't bias answers with your own thoughts or feelings.
3. Have people think aloud.	Ask people to verbally walk through a task as you record or take notes. Ask specific questions to get clarification. Tell them to say anything that comes into mind as they review plans and materials. Don't bias their answers with your own thoughts or feelings.
4. Use existing data.	Review usage and performance data to better understand the needs of people and the organization.

Which of these have you already tried? Which ways have helped you understand your audience the most?

I find that talking to people one-on-one and watching their work allows me to do methods 1–3 at the same time. Trying to do this in a group setting will almost always bias individual answers. It is critical that people know that we are looking for honest, "real" information and that nothing they do or say will cause problems.

Observing people work or use materials helps you understand what they use and don't use and *why they do what they do*. It helps you spot design problems that cause people to use workarounds. Watching and talking to several people shows you how people vary. For example, we often expect people to do certain things but, when we watch them, they do something entirely different

Prior knowledge, as we learned in Chapter 2, affects how people learn and what they understand. No two people learn exactly the same thing—even if they are hearing or seeing the same instruction.

For example, if you work for a car dealership that offers a monthly class that shows people how to get the most out of their new car, you could make a list of the types of questions and issues people have. You may note that different types of people ask different questions and have different concerns. You want to get the right information to the right type of person because people are generally not willing to read everything. (How many people read every manual they get? Very few. Thus, the warning "RTFM." Still, most won't.)

As instructional writers, we must know what different people need. And, because people have different levels of prior knowledge and different jobs, different groups of people most certainly need different things. We tune out information that has little relevance to our lives and work, because we are inundated with...

Too. Much. Information.

Tactic 2: Write for the Right Level of Prior Knowledge

What people already know is the very foundation of how we learn new information. Consider the times when someone has explained something to you and you didn't understand what they were talking about. For example, when my monitor wasn't working and my husband—an electrical engineer—started his discussion with electron flow. Huh? I barely know there are electrons, much less what they might have to do with my monitor. In other words, we must meet people where *they* are, not where *we* are.

When people in our audience know relatively little about the topic we are teaching, we need to go slower and help people understand what they are reading and hearing. This requires a lot more effort than most people realize.

In the car dealership's class, there will be people who only know how to drive their car (me) and people who feel comfortable working on their cars (my husband). When you tell us why different cars need different types of oil, I will not understand what you are talking about and my husband will already know this. Perhaps a smart dealership, after meeting this problem head-on a few times, will divide each group into *drivers* and *car nerds* so they can meet our different needs and talk to us differently.

Adults handle a lot of information daily. This becomes tiring and lowers our ability to handle difficulty. If we want people who deal with our instruction to understand, apply, and remember it, we must do everything we can to make it as learnable as possible.

Tactic 3: Make the Purpose Obvious

People want to know immediately if information pertains to them. If you get an email from human resources with the title "Holidays," you may save it for a time when you have less work to do—and, ultimately, not get around to reading it. If the same email has the title "Important Changes to Upcoming Holidays," you may open and read it at once because you want to know how it affects your plans.

We should use titles and introductory information that lets people know whether training and other performance materials are likely to meet their specific needs. Figure 3.2 shows a description of the training session at the dealership.

Figure 3.2 Dealership training description

Keep Yourself and Your New Car Happy After Purchase!
New cars keep getting more complex! Want to know how your new car works so you can take better care of it, make it last longer, and use the features you most want to use? We offer a free training class on [dates] from 6:30 to 8:30 PM.

Service techs and reps answer these questions and more. We will divide into groups to handle the types of questions you most want answered! Want to use the new tech features? Our touchscreen and tech guru has your answers. Want to talk shop? Our service techs gladly look under the hood and answer questions.

Email us or call us at…

The new car dealership started with a cutesy title for their course, but they realized that—with all the things flying across people's email and mail—people might not take the time to understand what the cutesy title meant.

Cutesy titles can gain attention. But it's a gamble. With instructional materials, most people want to figure out whether the content matches their needs—and titles help with this. Before using a funny or cute title, stop to consider the circumstances under which people will read it.

Will your audience take the time to understand it? A funny or cute title can work...or not. But make sure the description (and any other information that helps people decide whether it will meet their needs) is ridiculously obvious.

Tactic 4: Answer Audience Questions

We cannot simply push our desired information at our audience. They need to feel we have taken the time to understand their needs. One way we tell them we understand their needs is to answer their questions. Use the methods in Tactic 3 to find out what is important to them and what they want or need to know.

For example, at the dealership's new-car night, I have very basic questions.

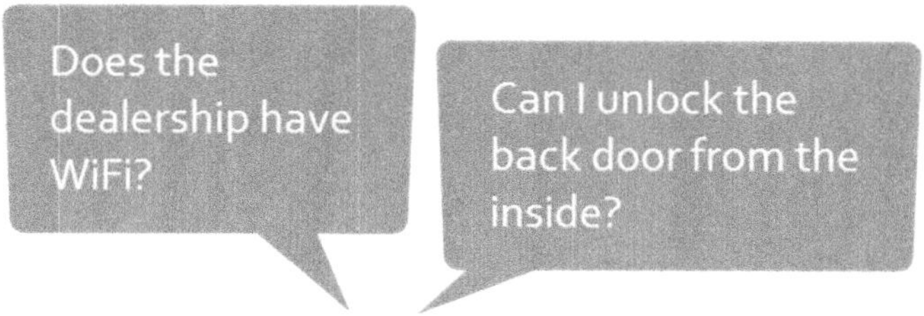

My husband has mechanical questions, so the dealership needs a very technically oriented person to answer them. He also dislikes certain features many cars have (like self-locking doors) and will want to know how to turn them off.

Technology offers all kinds of ways to answer questions if your class isn't face-to-face. And, when it comes to instruction, answering questions is one of the most critical services we provide. In fact, it's so important that, when possible, I like to find out what questions people have before I even begin developing instructional materials.

An audience that knows you care about its needs will be more interested in what you have to say.

Question: How did I decide *your* needs when writing this book? (Try to not look at my answers until you have formed your own answers.)
Answer: I used the experiences of people and clients I have worked with over many years. I talked to many people who write instructional materials. When I gave workshops and conference presentations, I listened for what people found most engaging and relevant. I also used a few experiences that bombed, so I knew what not to do. If you have questions I didn't answer or comments to make it better, do not hesitate to reach me. I'm listening!

Try It

We have reached the end of the tactics for **Strategy 1, Understand Your Audience's Needs.** Select instruction you want to or someone has asked you to build. Then use the tactics in this chapter (recapped below) to analyze the job context for this training.

Tactic 1	**Analyze Your Audience's Needs** Find out how what you are teaching intersects with the work your audience members do. What tasks are they doing when they apply the knowledge and skills? What kinds of problems come up that make it hard to apply the knowledge and skills? What is hard to do and how can this training help them? What would make the training most valuable to their work?
Tactic 2	**Write for the Right Level of Prior Knowledge** How much do potential audience members know about what you are teaching or designing? What content isn't valuable to them because they already know it or because it doesn't help them with the important parts of their job? What misconceptions do they have that you need to fix?
Tactic 3	**Make the Purpose Obvious** How will you let audience members know right away how training information pertains to their needs? How will you write titles and training information so they know whether training and materials are relevant to their needs and goals?
Tactic 4	**Answer Audience Questions** What questions do potential audience members have about what you are teaching or designing?

Consider doing this exercise with a group of people so you can discuss the following with others.

- What was helpful, less helpful?
- What did you learn?
- Which parts of this exercise will you continue to use in the future?

CHAPTER 4

Strategy 2: Write for Clarity

The goals of instructional writing are to help people learn, apply, and remember. Clarity is critical to these goals. Very clear instructional writing makes it easier and faster for people to understand instructional messages.

Clarity is also important for other kinds of writing, but it is even more important for instructional writing because instruction is often memory intensive.

Figure 4.1 lists seven tactics for making writing clearer. We will talk about each of them in Tactics 5 through 12.

Figure 4.1 Tactics that improve writing clarity

Tactic 5: Determine your key points
Tactic 6: Use shorter sentences
Tactic 7: Remove less valuable sentences
Tactic 8: Use simpler, more common words and phrases
Tactic 9: Talk directly to your reader or listener
Tactic 10: Prefer active voice
Tactic 11: Be direct about what people need to do
Tactic 12: Make long descriptions easier to understand

Tactic 5: Determine Your Key Points

Before we start writing, we should decide what we are writing about. Otherwise, we are likely to lose focus and simply keep adding information. This often ends up in messages that are unfocused and bloated.

We don't want to add content willy-nilly to instruction, as too much content can overload memory. Starting with a list of key points helps us stay focused. For example, in Figure 4.2, we see four key points for instruction on cybersecurity for small business.

Figure 4.2 Four key points for a small business cybersecurity course

1. There are costs for not protecting your business's information, including time and cost to mitigate damages, loss in confidence by customers and lost customers, litigation, and replacement of hardware and software.
2. There are different types of cybersecurity vulnerabilities and threats. Different practices reduce each type of threat and vulnerability.
3. Business owners must analyze their business's risk against each type of vulnerability and threat regularly.
4. If the risk level is high, business owners must figure out who in their business must follow which practices.

After deciding the key points, we must edit them as needed to make sure they are clear. For example, when writing the first key point in Figure 4.2, you might realize the message didn't make it clear that many of the costs for not protecting your business are *hidden*. Figure 4.3 shows changes made to the first key point to emphasize the hidden costs and to improve clarity.

Figure 4.3 Changes to first key point for small business cybersecurity course example

Before	After
There are costs for not protecting your business's information, including time and cost to mitigate damages, loss in confidence by customers and lost customers, litigation, and replacement of hardware and software.	There are obvious and hidden costs for not protecting your business's information, including ~~time and cost~~ hidden costs to ~~mitigate~~ reduce damages, loss in confidence by customers, ~~and~~ lost customers, possible litigation, and replacement of hardware and software.

Everything we write should be in service to the key points. If you find yourself adding more information outside the key points, you may have left out a key point. More likely, you are allowing yourself to add more content. Ask yourself:

- What is the key point for this extra content?
- Does it belong with the other key points, or is this getting bloated?

The less clear your content, the more explanation you may need to add. The more explanation, the less likely it is that people will find and remember your key points.

We know that the key points are clear when participants know what they are. For the course on cybersecurity for small business, the course asks participants to measure their business's risk against three specific threats. Before beginning the activity, the course asks participants to respond to a question to see if they know the reason (key point) for doing this activity (Figure 4.4). **Figure 4.4** Assessing whether participants know the key point

The reason for measuring your risk against these three threats is to:

A. Show that you know how to measure cybersecurity risk.

B. Analyze how much cybersecurity risk your business has.
C. Develop a template for how to measure cybersecurity risk.

Here is the output from the question, in a graph.

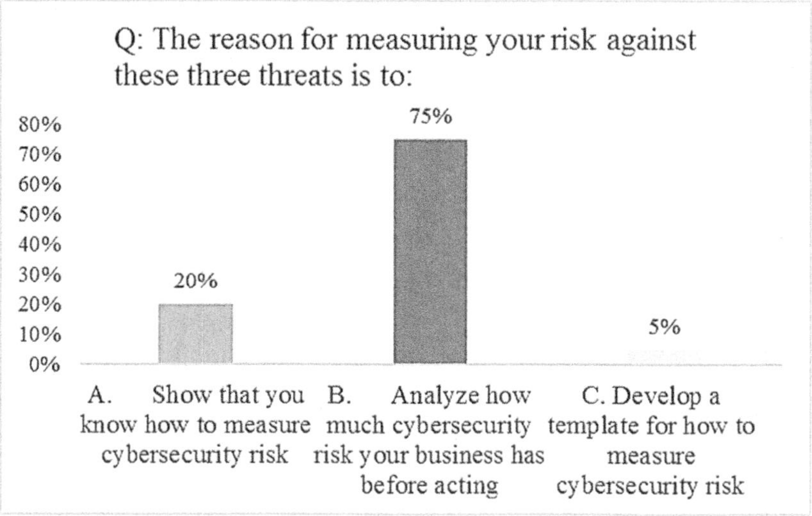

Question: Based on the results of the question, does the audience know the key point? (Try to not look at my answers until you have formed your own answers.)

Answer: The key point is B, Analyze how much cybersecurity risk your business has. Most people selected this answer, but 25% didn't. Because a quarter of the participants either didn't know or misunderstood this key point, we should make sure they understand.

I am in favor of a "mastery" approach to training. This means we should design training so everyone can master the desired knowledge and skills. Benjamin Bloom (yes, it's the person who developed Bloom's Taxonomy) proposed this instructional philosophy in 1968.

Tactic 6: Use Shorter Sentences

When sentences are longer than 15 to 20 words, people must use more mental effort to make sense of them. This is because they must piece together what the early part of the sentence says with what the later part says.

Review your longer sentences. Add periods and take out words to make shorter sentences (Figure 4.5). Reword for clarity if needed. Make your sentences clear and easier to read. You can vary sentence length, but make sure you have only one idea per sentence.

Figure 4.5 Examples of splitting longer sentences into shorter sentences *and* making them clearer

Before: To make sure we stay focused and don't add content willy-nilly to instruction (which is likely to overload memory), we can start with a list of key points or messages. (30 words)

After: We don't want to add content willy-nilly to instruction, as too much content can overload memory. (16 words)
or
Starting with a list of key points of messages helps us stay focused. (13 words)

\-\-\-

Before: Look at your longer sentences, and add periods and take out words to see if splitting them into shorter sentences makes them easier to read and more clear. (28 words)

After: Review your longer sentences. (4 words)
or
Add periods and take out words to make shorter sentences. (10 words.)

Counting the number of words in your sentences is tedious. If you use Microsoft Word, it can count words for you. If you are using another writing tool, see if it offers ways to do word counts.

Resource: Number of Words Using Microsoft Word (Windows)

To count the number of words in a sentence in Microsoft Word:

1. Select the sentence you want to check.
2. Look at the lower-left side of the Word window. You will see the number of words selected (Figure 4.6). Your version may be somewhat different, so search the help files for "word count."

Figure 4.6 Number of words selected

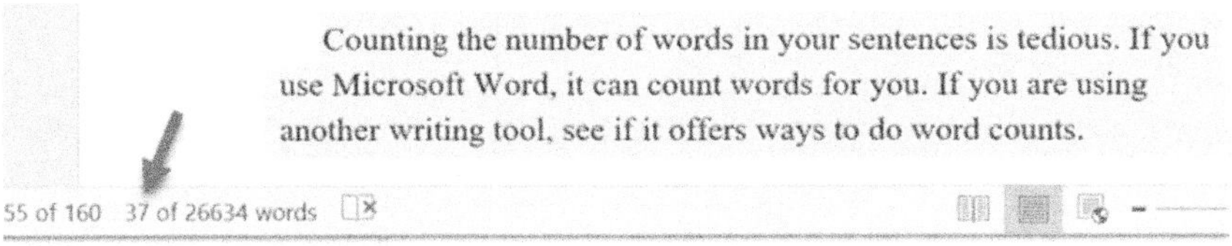

Tactic 7: Remove Less-Valuable Sentences

When an editor reads written materials, he or she can see there is "stuff" that doesn't add to the message. Without an editor, we need to get good at finding this stuff and taking it out. Our sentences and paragraphs need to be lean and clear.

Figure 4.7 shows the process of editing a paragraph from wordy to less wordy and more clear. The final (edited) paragraph offers clear guidelines that are hard to find in the wordy initial paragraph.

Figure 4.7 Edits to a wordy paragraph

Initial paragraph (99 words):
When sentences are longer than 15 to 20 words, people need more mental effort to make sense of them. That increases the cognitive load. Look at your longer sentences. Do they need to be that long or could they be shorter? Add periods and take out words to make shorter sentences. Now read them and see if they aren't clearer when they are shorter and have fewer words. You'll probably agree, once you're used to being ruthless with words, that this makes them easier to read and more clear. Vary sentence length, but have only one idea per sentence.

Select sentences to remove:
When sentences are longer than 15 to 20 words, people need more mental effort to make sense of them. That increases the cognitive load. ~~Look at your longer sentences. Do they need to be that long or could they be shorter?~~ Add periods and take out words to make shorter sentences. ~~Now read them and see if they aren't clearer when they are shorter and have fewer words. You'll probably agree, once you're used to being ruthless with words, that this~~ That makes them easier to read and more clear. Vary sentence length, but have only one idea per sentence.

Remove sentences and rewrite for clarity (58 words):
When sentences are longer than 15 to 20 words, people need more mental effort to make sense of them. That increases the cognitive load. Look at your longer sentences. Add periods and take out words to make shorter sentences. This makes them easier to read and more clear. Vary sentence length, but have only one idea per sentence.

Question: How do you decide which sentences to remove?

Answer: Here's what I do. I read my paragraphs and find the key message and the sentences that support it. I then remove sentences that seem redundant or unnecessary. I re-read my paragraphs. If the meaning is unchanged and the main message is now clearer (because there are fewer words), I leave those sentences out.

I often need multiple rounds of editing because clarity is so critical to instruction. There are times when I find that entire paragraphs add little. It has taken me many years to feel good about cutting many paragraphs or sections of content—especially ones that took me a while to write—simply because they weren't valuable. (Before I do massive cuts, I always save a copy in case I realize I'm wrong or that I need those paragraphs elsewhere.)

Tactic 8: Use Simpler, More Common Words and Phrases

Many people use complex words and phrases because they think it makes them sound more knowledgeable. But complex words and phrases reduce readability, which makes content less learnable. Plain-language research shows that simpler and more conversational language is easier to read and understand.

Let's review an example (Figure 4.8) to see how using less-complex language makes it easier to understand instructions.

Figure 4.8 National Marine Fisheries Service, National Oceanic and Atmosphere Administration, Quick-Reference Card Language (Source: http://www.plainlanguage.gov/examples/before_after/regfisheries.cfm)

Before (68 words)	**After** (18 words
After notification of NMFS, this final rule requires all CA/OR DGN vessel operators to have attended one Skipper Education Workshop after all workshops have been convened by NMFS in September 1997. CA/OR DGN vessel operators are required to attend Skipper Education Workshops at annual intervals thereafter, unless that requirement is waived by NMFS. NMFS will provide sufficient notice to vessel operators by mail prior to convening workshops.	After notification from NMFS, vessel operators must attend a Skipper education workshop before commencing fishing each fishing season.

My goodness. The After example can be simpler still. How about this instead?

NMFS will notify vessel operators to attend a mandatory Skipper education workshop before they start fishing each season. (18 words)

Figure 4.9 shows another example.

Figure 4.9 Choosing a ladder example (Source: www.osha.gov/dte/outreach/construction/focus_four?falls/fallhaz_handouts.pdf)

Choose the right ladder for the job. (87 words)
– First, you need to make sure that a ladder is the best equipment for what you need to do. Would scaffolding or a mechanical lift be better?
– Many times, the ladder is the only physical support you have while you are working. If it fails, you can fall. That's why it is so important to find the right ladder when you do need to use one. The three main types of ladders—step ladders, straight ladders, and extension ladders—are used in different situations for different tasks.

Here's my suggested rewrite.

Choose the right ladder for the job. (45 words)
It's important to make sure you have the right equipment to be safe. A ladder can be the only thing holding you up. If it fails, you're injured or worse. Ask yourself: Is a ladder the right equipment for this task? Which kind of ladder?

If you read aloud and it doesn't sound like something you'd say in everyday conversation, it's too complex. Once you start looking for complex language, practice editing the language to simplify the wording. How do you find the right simpler words and phrases to use? I will show you two good resources next.

Resource: Plain Language Word and Phrase Substitution List

The Plain Language site (www.plainlanguage.gov) offers a list of complex words and phrases paired with simpler words and phrases you can use instead. Figure 4.10 shows a sample of their Simple Words and Phrases section.

Figure 4.10 Words and phrases from the Simple Words and Phrases List (www.plainlanguage.gov/howto/wordsuggestions/simplewords.cfm), slightly adapted

Instead of using this complex word or phrase	Use this simpler word or phrase
commence	begin, start
implement	carry out, start
in accordance with	by, following, per, under
in order that	for, so
in the event of	if
in view of	since
it is	(omit)
maintain	keep
monitor	watch
notify	tell
objective	goal
option	choice
perform	do
preclude	prevent
remain	stay
solicit	ask for, request
the use of	(omit)
utilize	use

Instead of using this complex word or phrase	Use this simpler word or phrase
whereas	because
witnessed	saw

The United States government developed the Plain Language site for written government communications. Why not go through your information and training and see what complex words you use too often? Then plan to replace those words with simpler words. One warning! Be careful about using Find and Replace without looking at each word you are replacing. You can mistakenly replace some wrong words this way. I know because I have done it with disastrous results.

Resource: Wordiness List

Dr. G. Kim Blank from the Department of English at the University of Victoria, Canada (remember that Canada, Great Britain, Australia, the USA, and other English-speaking countries have differences in English usage), offers a Wordiness List (http://web.uvic.ca/~gkblank/wordiness.html) and recommends avoiding these phrases:

- it is/was
- there is/are/was/were
- that is/are/was/were
- which is/are/was/were
- who is/are/was/were

He also recommends getting rid of what he calls "fuzzy words," such as entirely, extremely, literally, overall, perfectly, ultimately, and others.

Dr. Blank offers an A through Z list of words and phrases to avoid. This list is more comprehensive than the Plain Language Simple Words and Phrases list. This is a terrific resource you will find invaluable. Bookmark it.

Question: Should we always use simpler, conversational language?

Answer: Most of the time it's the best approach. But remember Tactic 1: Analyze Your Audience's Needs. You must decide what is best for your audience.

Don't use technical terms or jargon unless you know people expect and understand them. If you do use them, it's generally a good idea to define technical terms as you come to them when writing for less-expert audiences.

There is often an added problem with content written by experts, and it can be overwhelming. Experts tend to focus too much on what *they* know and too little on what the audience needs to know and do. If you are an expert, concentrate on audience questions, problems, and job issues, and focus on giving your audience members the information *they* need for what they need to be able to do. Don't allow your love of details to overwhelm less-technical or less-expert audiences.

Question: This could take a lot of time. Are there ways to make it faster and easier?

Answer: I know the complex words and phrases I tend to overuse, and I keep a list of them and the best alternatives. This makes me more aware of my writing habits. I also set up Word to find complex words and passive sentences. You will see how to do this in Tactic 10.

Tactic 9: Talk Directly to Your Reader or Listener

You should consider your writing a discussion between you and the person reading or listening to it. Not *all people* reading or listening to it—*each* person reading or listening to it. In instructional writing, we call this the "personalization principle," which holds that conversational writing is better than formal writing for learning.

No one likes to be addressed as *Dear applicant* or *Dear student*! Use *you* and *we* (Table 4.1). And check that it passes the conversation test. Remember the final skipper education language in Tactic 8:

> NMFS will notify vessel operators to attend a mandatory Skipper education workshop before they start fishing each season.

We can make it even more friendly and conversational like this.

> NMFS will let you know when you need to attend the Skipper education workshop before you start fishing each season.

Table 4.1 Impersonal sentences and rewrites to make them more personal

Impersonal	**Personal**
• Advice about funding can be secured from...	Ask us for advice about funding...
• In accordance with last week's memo, time off should be...	When taking time off, you should...
• The company has requirements that all staff...	We need you to...
• Make sure vendors are apprised when...	We want you to let vendors know when...

Tactic 10: Prefer Active Voice

If you are an English language geek, you may realize that some of the stuffy and hard-to-understand phrases we've looked at are examples of passive voice. Passive voice makes the subject of the sentence unclear.

Most sentences have three main parts:

a **subject** (the noun who does the action)

a **verb** (the action)

an **object** (who or what received the action)

Here is a sentence written in active voice.

I	**wrote**	this **book.** (4 words)
subject	verb	object

Here's the same sentence in passive voice.

This **book**	**was written**	by **me.** (6 words)
object	verb	subject

In active voice, the subject of the sentence does the action. It is far less clear who does the action in passive voice. Figuring this out uses mental effort. Most workers are busy and, if they must work to understand, they will skip over, guess, or misunderstand. Active voice is simpler and clearer. We should use it in most cases.

Look at the examples in Table 4.2 to see whether the passive or active version is clearer—and how many words it takes to communicate the point. The first two are *there is/it is* examples. Remember that Dr. Blank's Wordiness List, one of the resources we discussed in Tactic 8, tells us we shouldn't start sentences with *there is* or *it is/was.*

Table 4.2 Rewrites of passive sentences to active sentences

Passive	Active
1. There is a safety video that must be viewed by every staff member every year. (15 words)	You must view a safety video each year. (8 words)
2. It is better to notify your supervisor about vacation time as far in advance as you can. (17 words)	You should notify your supervisor about vacation time as far in advance as possible. (14 words)
3. The policies were put into place after gathering input from departments. (11 words)	We gathered departmental input before implementing the policies. (8 words)
4. The matter of unpaid leave will be discussed shortly. (9 words)	We will discuss unpaid leave shortly. (6 words)

Some people will tell you not to use passive voice anywhere. But passive voice makes sense when you don't know who is responsible or when you don't want to reveal who is responsible—as when you're telling a mystery story.

Passive voice also makes sense when you need to write in a non-threatening way. For example, it may be preferable to write, for quiz or test question feedback, "The final score wasn't quite high enough (75/100). Try again?" (passive voice) rather than "You didn't get a passing score (75/100). Try again?" (active voice).

If you don't write in active voice, you may have difficulty finding it in your writing. Microsoft Word can make this easier for you, and I describe how that works next. If you use other tools for writing, see if they have features that help you find passive sentences.

Resource: Passive Sentences Finder, Microsoft Word (Windows)

In many later versions of Microsoft Word, you can select an option to find passive sentences. It is under Word Options with Spelling and Grammar. Different versions of Microsoft Word handle this differently, so you may need to use help to find it (search for "passive sentences").

Figure 4.11 shows you how to select the passive voice options in Word Options. Figure 4.12 shows you how passive sentences appear in your text and what happens when you right-click a passive sentence. Generally, you will simply need to rewrite the sentence to start with the subject of the sentence.

Figure 4.11 Selecting passive voice in Word Options

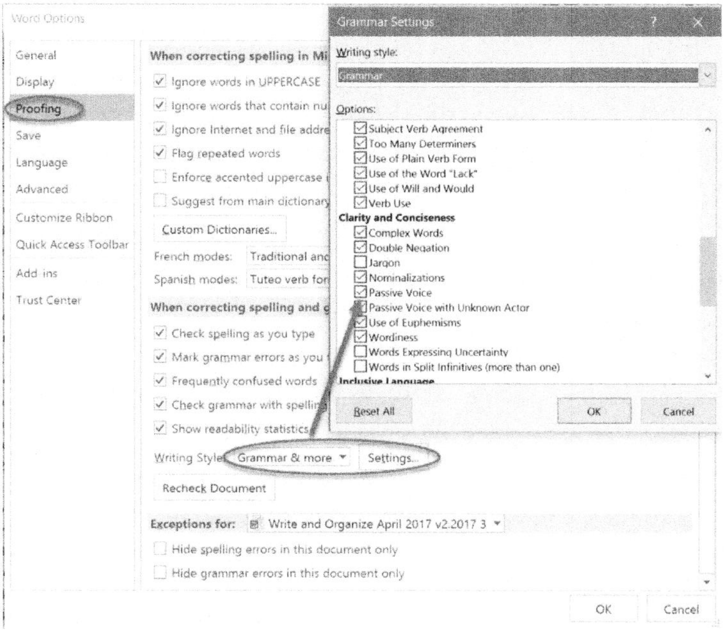

Figure 4.12 How passive text appears after right-clicking it

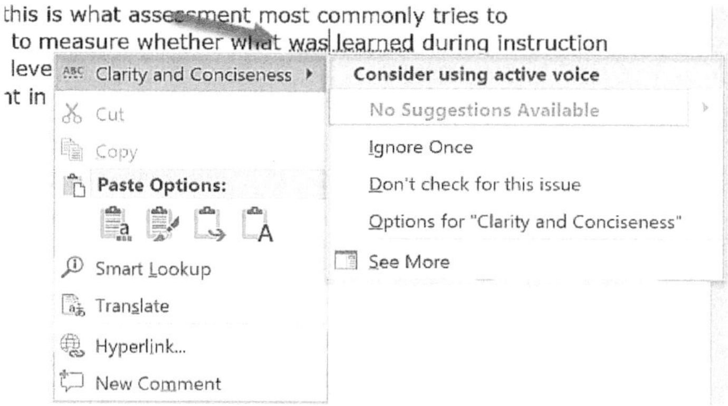

About Using Grammar Checkers (and Spell-Check)

If you search online for "problems with grammar checkers," you'll find that grammar and spell checkers have many limitations and problems.

Problems include seeing acceptable grammar as bad and not finding problems in unacceptable grammar. This is true in MS Word's grammar checks, as well, as noted by Daniel Kies, of the English department of the College of DuPage, who analyzed grammar checkers, including Word's, on 20 of the most common grammatical problems in college papers (http://papyr.com/hypertextbooks/grammar/gramchek.htm).

While you might use them (I do), don't count on them. I hire a professional editor for my most important writing. I may use grammar checkers, but I know they have serious flaws. I also know I will not find errors in my own work. Plus, almost all writers have an added flaw: We fall in love with our words, which I'm sorry to say is unacceptable. Someone once told me we should ruthlessly edit our own work as if someone we don't like or respect had written it!

My editor told me that the more complex the sentences, the more likely it is that grammar checkers will make mistakes. She said grammar checkers are notoriously wrong with dialogue, quotes or citations, and non-traditionally formatted work. It should be obvious that neither grammar checkers nor spell checkers have any ability to tell if what you wrote makes sense. And they absolutely cannot tell if what you wrote will make sense for your audience.

Resource: Pro Writing Aid

Spelling and grammar tools cannot take the place of a good editor, period. If you have limited funds, spend them on an editor. But there is a tool that can help you find problems and improve your writing. I've tried several tools and found them dreadful. Until I read about Pro Writing Aid on a writing blog and tried it out, prepared to be unhappy. I wasn't! It helps me find:

- Words I overuse
- Sentences that don't vary in length (they should) or are too long (too hard to read), without having to check each sentence's length manually
- Lazy writing (overuse of common words)
- Overused pronouns
- Readability
- Inconsistencies in spelling (such as job-aid and job aid)

Pro Writing Aid works in Mac and Windows and works as a web tool and as an add-on to Microsoft Word. It has a free version and various paid versions. I bought the Premium Lifetime version because, as an instructional writer, I know I will use it a lot. You can find a URL below and a code for 25% off the Premium Lifetime version in case you want to use it, too. But at least give the free version a try.

https://prowritingaid.com
CODE (25% off Premium Lifetime): SHANK

Tactic 11: Be Direct About What People Need to Do

Instructional writers are often indirect when telling people what they need to do. But clear expectations or directions are helpful, especially in instructional writing. Having to make sense of vague text creates added mental effort. And there's more chance that people will guess wrong.

For example, Figure 4.13 shows a screen from a food safety course. Although the text indicates what to do, it doesn't clearly say, *Do these specific things*.

Figure 4.13 Hand-washing safety screen with unspecific directions

When we need people to do specific things, we should clearly tell them what they need to do and how they need to do it (Figure 4.14).

Figure 4.14 Hand-washing safety screen with specific directions

In Figure 4.15, I offer more examples that show unclear, indirect language and how to make it more clear and direct. While I was fiddling with directness, I also made passive sentences active, shortened sentences, and used more familiar words.

Figure 4.15 Examples of unclear and indirect language made clear and direct

Unclear, indirect language	**Clear, direct language**
1. It is advised that you read all of the documents prior to signing them, as they contain information of importance to your benefits.	You should read the documents before signing them. They include important information about your benefits.
2. It is easier to make changes before the final piece is put into place.	Make all changes before you put the final piece into place.

Tactic 12: Make Long Descriptions Easier to Understand

Long descriptions can take a lot of mental effort to understand. Ways of reducing mental effort with long descriptions include:

1. Making the text more concise
2. Replacing the text with a graphic
3. A combination of 1 and 2

In Figure 4.16, I show an expert's dense text about how to use a personal fire extinguisher, and then a rewritten and very concise version of that text.

Figure 4.16 Before-and-after examples of making dense descriptions concise

Before

When using a personal fire extinguisher, there are really only four steps. We teach people to remember the four steps by using the phrase PASS. Here is what each of the letters mean. Most fire extinguishers have a safety pin in the handle with a plastic seal. You need to break the seal and pull the pin before you can use the fire extinguisher. So, the first thing you need to do is PULL the pin on the extinguisher. You can't use the fire extinguisher until the pin has been pulled out. Then you must AIM the hose's nozzle at the base of the flames. To start the fire extinguisher's agent, you SQUEEZE the handle. The agent starts to be released. Then you need to SWEEP the nozzle of the fire extinguisher from side to side. Do this at the base of the flames until the fire is extinguished.

It is very important to decide if you have enough time to get out before using the fire extinguisher. Most full, small fire extinguishers have 10 or fewer seconds of extinguishing power. If you cannot put the fire out in that amount of time, you should get yourself and others to safety rather than try to put the fire out. And if there is a lot of smoke, get out quickly.

After (1)
How to use a small fire extinguisher: **P A S S**
PULL the pin on the extinguisher.
AIM the nozzle of the hose at the base of the flames.
SQUEEZE the handle to start the flow.
SWEEP the nozzle from side to side at the base of the flames to extinguish the flames.

You may have noticed that the concise text was too concise to supply all the necessary details. But rather than bombard people with all the details (which may be hard to understand when delivered at once), we can supply a concise core and then add more details, as you see in Figure 4.17.

Figure 4.17 Concise text, quiz questions to check for understanding, added concise details

After (2)

How to use a small fire extinguisher: **P A S S**

PULL the pin on the extinguisher.

AIM the nozzle of the hose at the base of the flames.

SQUEEZE the handle to start the flow.

SWEEP the nozzle from side to side at the base of the flames to extinguish the flames.

Question: The acronym PASS helps us remember what to do when using a fire extinguisher. What does each letter stand for? (Select the correct word for each letter of the acronym.)

P	Press Place Pull*
A	Access Aim* All
S	Squeeze* Simple Several
S	Select Sweep* Specialized

* correct answer

Wait. Should you fight that fire?

It is very important to decide if you have enough time to get out before using the fire extinguisher. Most full, small fire extinguishers have 10 or fewer seconds of extinguishing power. If you cannot put the fire out in that amount of time, you should get yourself and others to safety rather than try to put the fire out. And if there is a lot of smoke, get out quickly.

There are times when you shouldn't use a fire extinguisher. If there's a lot of smoke or the fire is progressing quickly, you should get yourself and others out *right away* and NOT use a fire extinguisher.

Fire extinguishers hold a very limited amount of fire-fighting agent. Use an extinguisher only if it is safe and you can quickly put the fire out.

Question: When should we ***not*** apply the actions specified in PASS? (Select the best answer.)

A. We should remember what PASS means and always apply the actions.

B. We should first get everyone else out of the building and then use the actions specified in PASS.

C. We shouldn't try to put out the fire if there's a lot of smoke or we can't quickly put out the fire. *

* correct answer

Figure 4.18 shows the third technique: making the description visual along with concise text. Using graphics rather than text fits a lot of content into a small amount of space. Instead of a long description, it shows a portable fire extinguisher and concise text that explains the four steps of PASS. The reader clicks on the numbers 1-2-3-4 to get added information (each pop-up explains one part of the acronym).

Figure 4.18 Example of visual + concise text

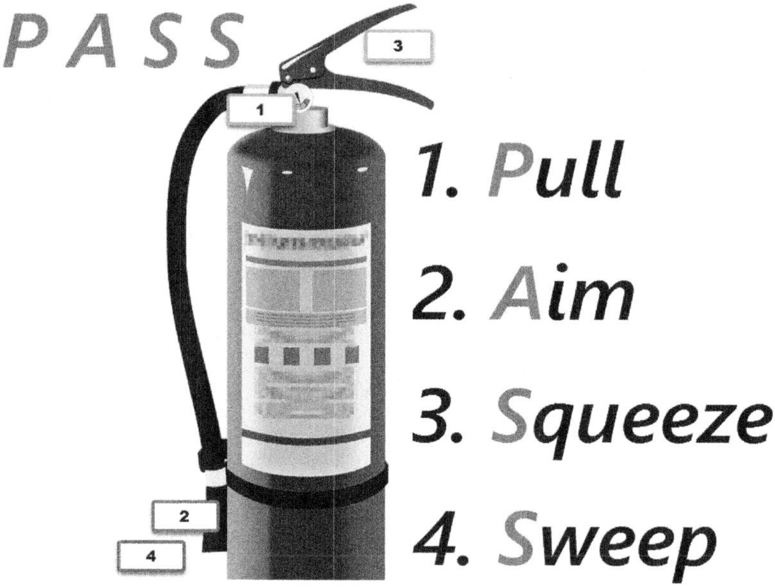

Graphics standing in for text descriptions make sense when the description is *naturally visual*. For example, illustrations that show the many different types of USB (Universal Serial Bus) connectors, or graphs showing changes to birth rates over time. It also makes content easier to remember. If a visual is self-explanatory, don't *add* an explanation. Simply add a caption and alt text for those with impaired sight or hearing.

Allan Paivio, a professor at the University of Western Ontario, and Douglas Nelson, Professor Emeritus at the University of South Florida, did research that helps us understand the way we process images. The fact that we remember images more easily than text is called the "picture superiority effect." Pictures are more perceptually distinctive than words. This makes them easier to remember.

Research also shows that graphics that are there just to add visuals to a page often waste mental energy, so it is better that we not use them in instruction. In another Make It Learnable book I will discuss what research says about using various media.

The following are important learning principles for using graphics.

DO	DON'T
✓ When a graphic needs explanation, use *audio* narration for better understanding. You should supply a transcript or captioning for those who need it.	X Don't add graphics for the sake of adding graphics. Pointless graphics add pointless mental effort.
✓ If a graphic needs an explanation, put the explanation with the graphic.	

Next, I offer suggestions for practicing the tactics in this strategy. Research tells us that practicing, especially in a realistic manner, will cement these skills for you.

Don't forget that you can practice these tactics any time you write or organize instruction. Go to the checklist at the end of the book and analyze which tactics are most needed. Then use the information in the book until you can teach the tactics to others!

Try It

We have reached the end of the tactics for **Strategy 2, Write for Clarity.** Select instruction you want to or someone has asked you to build. Then use the tactics in this chapter (recapped below) to make the content more learnable.

Tactic 5	**Determine Your Key Points** Start by determining the key points and writing to them. Or find the key points. Does the writing veer from them? If so, analyze which content to remove and which messages need to be more noticeable.
Tactic 6	**Use Shorter Sentences** Divide your longer sentences into shorter sentences.
Tactic 7	**Remove Less-Valuable Sentences** Look for sentences that don't add anything or repeat what you have already said and remove them.
Tactic 8	**Use Simpler, More Common Words and Phrases** Use the Plain Language Simple Words and Phrases list or Dr. Blank's Wordiness List to replace complex words and phrases with simpler words and phrases.
Tactic 9	**Talk Directly to Your Reader or Listener** Change wording to make it sound as if you are talking directly to the reader. Use *you* and *we*. Make your language more conversational and friendly.
Tactic 10	**Prefer Active Voice** Use active voice. Turn on Microsoft Word's passive sentences finder and search for passive sentences. Make them active.
Tactic 11	**Be Direct About What People Need to Do** Tell your reader what they need to do. Don't make them figure it out!
Tactic 12	**Make Long Descriptions Easier to Understand** Can any be more concise or replaced with a graphic?

Consider doing this exercise with a group of people so you can discuss the following with others.

- What was helpful, less helpful?
- What did you learn?
- Which parts of this exercise will you continue to use in the future?

CHAPTER 5

Strategy 3: Make Text Readable and Legible

In this strategy, I discuss making content readable and legible. I discussed readability in Chapter 2, in the section "Learnability." And, in Chapter 4, I discussed tactics for improving the comprehension of content. How we present text also affects readability. Many of the following tactics fall under the term "legibility." Figure 5.1 lists the design tactics that make text legible, or able to be read. We talk about them in Tactics 13 through 20.

Figure 5.1 Tactics that make text easier to read

Tactic 13: Test Readability
Tactic 14: Use Readable Fonts
Tactic 15: Use Readable Type Sizes
Tactic 16: Left-align Body Text
Tactic 17: Use Adequate White Space
Tactic 18: Space Lines of Text for Ease of Reading
Tactic 19: Use readable line lengths
Tactic 20: Offer adequate contrast between text and background

Tactic 13: Test Readability

In Chapter 2, I discussed using readability scores to figure out if the intended audience will find the content readable. Next, I'll show you how to do readability calculations using Microsoft Word.

Resource: Readability Statistics in Microsoft Word (Windows)

Later versions of Microsoft Word (typically under Word Options, in Windows) include readability statistics called Flesch Reading Ease (Figure 5.2). Depending on the version of Word you use, it may look slightly different from what you see below.

In the versions of Word I have recently used, the readability statistics appear after you spell-check the entire document. Your version might do something different.

Figure 5.2 Readability statistics from Word Options

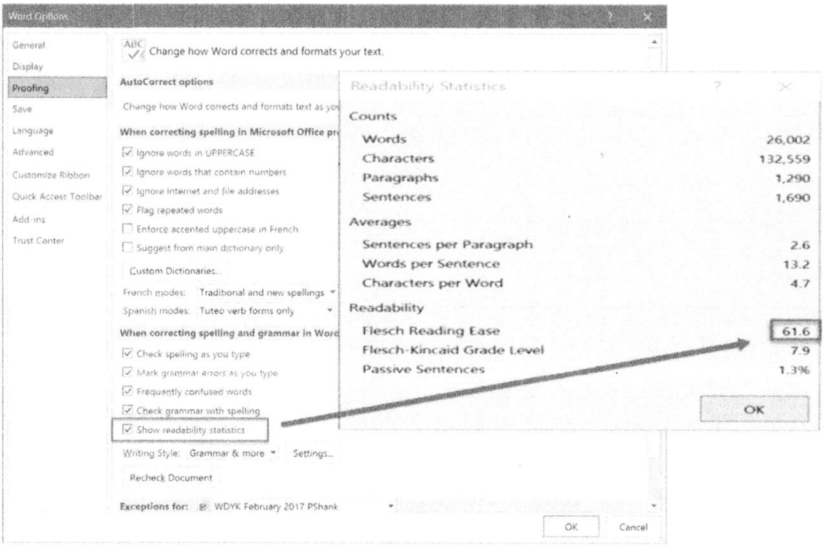

There are other readability statistics and other tools you can use to check readability. Flesch Reading Ease is one of the most common readability scores, and it rates text on a 100-point scale. The higher the score, the easier the text is to understand. For best understanding with a typical audience, a score of 60 to 70 is ideal (see Table 2.1).

There Are Many Readability Scores

I selected Flesch Reading Ease because it is the readability score Word calculates. But a lot of people use other readability scores. One readability score that comes up often is the SMOG Readability Formula, which estimates the years of education a person needs to understand the writing. SMOG stands for Simple Measure of Gobbledygook (delightful!), and G. Harry McLaughlin created it to improve on other readability formulas.

It is easy to calculate SMOG using a calculator. If you are interested in learning more, here is a good resource: http://www.learningandwork.org.uk/SMOG-calculator/smogcalc.php. McLaughlin explains his method (adapted from *SMOG Grading—New Readability Formula*):

1. In the text you want to assess, select a group of 10 consecutive sentences near the beginning of the text, 10 consecutive sentences in the middle, and 10 consecutive sentences near the end.
2. In the 30 sentences you selected, count every word of three or more syllables. If a word with three or more syllables is repeated, count each repetition.
3. Take the square root of the nearest perfect square (perfect squares: 5x5=25, 6x6=36, 7x7=49, 8x8=64, 9x9=81, 10x10=100, 11X11=121, 12x12=144, etc.). If the count is 95, the nearest perfect square is 100 and the square root is 10. If the count lies between two perfect squares, choose the lower number.
4. Add 3 to the number in Step 3. This gives the SMOG Grade. This is the reading grade of a person who can understand the text.

Readability Scores Can Be Problematic

Readability is just a start for figuring out whether people can understand your materials. Although I recommend testing readability, testing itself is not enough. Readability scores assume longer words are more difficult than shorter words and that words with more syllables are more difficult than words with fewer syllables. This may not be the case if the longer words and words with more syllables are familiar to your audience and the shorter words and words with fewer syllables are new to them.

Readability scores are based on generic audiences. Your audience is not generic, so you need to use what you know about them. The National Assessment of Adult Literacy found that reading level is often *below* the last grade a person completed. The words someone uses and understands often depend on several factors, including demographics and their job. If you are writing training materials on putting out fires in the home, for example, the wording will probably need to be different for children and teens, homeowners, and property management staff. Training materials for fire professionals will use words other audiences are unlikely to understand. You cannot simply depend on readability formulas. Consider it a place to start.

If the reading level is too difficult, ask:

- What does the audience know about this topic?
- How clear are the materials to someone who knows what you think they know? Can you test these assumptions with members of the audience?
- What words do audience members use in everyday language? Do most know what the words you are using mean?
- Will writing more simply make reading, application, and understanding easier?

Readability may be important, but, by itself, it isn't enough. Real readability means knowing your audience and writing *for them*.

Tactic 14: Use Readable Fonts

Font fanatics and readability experts debate the legibility of serif fonts (fonts with small decorative embellishments, such as Times) versus sans serif fonts (fonts without those embellishments, such as Arial).

Some say we should use serif fonts in print-based materials and sans serif fonts in digital materials. Research is unclear, so we can assume (for now) there is no significant difference between the readability of serif fonts and that of sans serif fonts in either print or digital.

Luckily, research does offer the following guidance for choosing fonts for readability. We should:

- Use fonts that are non-decorative, not unusual, and unlikely to convey specific meanings.
- Make text large enough to read in the selected medium. The farther away the text will be from the reader, the larger it needs to be.
- Use sentence case (normal upper- and lowercase) because it is easier to read than UPPERCASE (Figure 5.3).
- Use UPPERCASE, **bold**, or *italics* only for emphasis, as they are harder to read, and we should not overuse them.
- Use only one or two fonts.

Figure 5.3 Body text in sentence case (top), uppercase (middle), and italics (bottom)

You cannot use this method to add a caption to lists. If you build a complex list with headings, you can put lists inside a table, remove the borders, and then add a caption.

YOU CANNOT USE THIS METHOD TO ADD A CAPTION TO LISTS. IF YOU BUILD A COMPLEX LIST WITH HEADINGS, YOU CAN PUT LISTS INSIDE A TABLE, REMOVE THE BORDERS, AND THEN ADD A CAPTION.

You cannot use this method to add a caption to lists. If you build a complex list with headings, you can put lists inside a table, remove the borders, and then add a caption.

Tactic 15: Use Readable Type Sizes

We measure type on a computer screen in point sizes. Linda Lohr, who was an instructional technology professor and is the author of *Creating Graphics for Learning and Performance*, recommends that non-projected (printed and computer) text (for example, articles, job aids, and online courses) be around 12 points.

It is difficult to offer hard-and-fast rules about point sizes, however, as different typefaces in the same point size are often different sizes, as you can see in Figure 5.4. Look at how much space the different typefaces take up in the same point size. Arial and Courier New almost look too big, while Garamond looks reasonably sized for a print page (...to my eyes. How about you?).

Figure 5.4 Different typefaces in the same size: Arial 12 (top), Courier New 12 (middle), and Garamond 12 (bottom)

You cannot use this method to add a caption to lists. If you build a complex list with headings, you can put lists inside a table, remove the borders, and then add a caption.

\---

You cannot use this method to add a caption to lists. If you build a complex list with headings, you can put lists inside a table, remove the borders, and then add a caption.

\---

You cannot use this method to add a caption to lists. If you build a complex list with headings, you can put lists inside a table, remove the borders, and then add a caption.

Style sheets (for computer text) can allow readers to change the size of text on their screen. Consider adding the option to increase or decrease the text size for those who need it.

For projected text (such as slides on a screen), text must be much larger. Normally 18 points is the very smallest projected text size people can read; however, 18 points may be far too small from the back of a large auditorium. This means that, to know what will work, you need to test projected text at the size people will view it. And text will look quite different when viewed from either the front or back of a large room. Yes, a dilemma. Ask yourself where people are most likely to sit. In the conferences I attend, more people sit in the middle and the back.

Tactic 16: Left-Align Body Text

For English body text, many sources recommend using left-aligned, rather than justified, body text. This is because left-aligned text is easier to read than justified text (Figure 5.5). Justifying the text varies the spacing between words on each line of text. The equal spacing in left-aligned text keeps thoughts that go together more visually united. Many sources also recommend that we not split words (hyphenating) over two lines, for the same reason.

Figure 5.5 Justified text and left-aligned text

Justified body text

There are debates about whether serif fonts (fonts with small decorative embellishments, such as Times) or sans serif fonts (fonts without embellishments, such as Arial) are easier to read, especially in longer text passages. Some say we should use serif fonts in print-based materials and sans serif fonts in digital materials.

Research has shown no significant difference between the readability of serif fonts and sans serif fonts in either medium.

Left-aligned body text

There are debates about whether serif fonts (fonts with small decorative embellishments, such as Times) or sans serif fonts (fonts without embellishments, such as Arial) are easier to read, especially in longer text passages. Some say we should use serif fonts in print-based materials and sans serif fonts in digital materials.

Research has shown no significant difference between the readability of serif fonts and sans serif fonts in either medium.

Tactic 17: Use Adequate White Space

White space—the parts of a page that have nothing on them (such as margins, space between columns and lines of type, and space around graphics)—makes it easier for people to see the organization of the content. In instruction, we need to communicate not only content, but also how the content pieces relate to each other.

Cluttered and densely packed content makes the organization of the content hard to perceive. This type of page layout also tends to make content look difficult and unappealing. In Figure 5.6, we see the same dummy content spaced densely (the top example) and with more white space (the bottom example). The bottom example looks less difficult, and we more easily notice the headings because there is more white space.

Figure 5.6 Densely spaced headings and text (top) and more widely spaced headings and text (bottom)

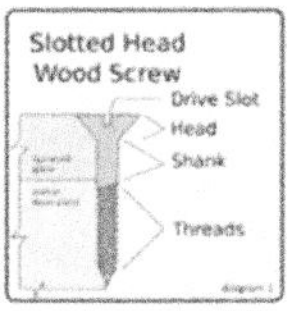

Lorem ipsum dolor
Aenean commodo ligula eget dolor. Aenean massa. Cum sociis natoque penatibus et magnis dis parturient montes, nascetur ridiculus mus.
Donec quam felis
Nulla consequat massa quis enim. Donec pede justo, fringilla vel, aliquet nec, vulputate eget, arcu. In enim justo, rhoncus ut, imperdiet a, venenatis vitae, justo. Nullam dictum felis eu pede mollis pretium. Integer tincidunt.

Lorem ipsum dolor

Aenean commodo ligula eget dolor. Aenean massa. Cum sociis natoque penatibus et magnis dis parturient montes, nascetur ridiculus mus.

Donec quam felis

Nulla consequat massa quis enim. Donec pede justo, fringilla vel, aliquet nec, vulputate eget, arcu. In enim justo, rhoncus ut, imperdiet a, venenatis vitae, justo. Nullam dictum felis eu pede mollis pretium. Integer tincidunt.

Tactic 18: Space Lines of Text for Ease of Reading

Line spacing is the distance from the base of one line of text to the base of another line of text (Figure 5.7).

Figure 5.7 Line spacing

Lorem ipsum dolor sit amet, consectetuer adipiscing elit. Aenean commodo ligula eget dolor. Aenean massa. Cum sociis natoque

We can read lines of text more easily when we don't space them too closely together or too far apart (Figure 5.8). When we space them too closely together, text is hard to read. When we space them too far apart, readers must search for the next line and decide whether the lines belong together. Too much work!

Figure 5.8 Text spaced too closely (top), appropriately (middle), and too far apart (bottom)

You cannot use this method to add a caption to lists. If you build a complex list with headings, you can put lists inside a table, remove the borders, and then add a caption.

You cannot use this method to add a caption to lists. If you build a complex list with headings, you can put lists inside a table, remove the borders, and then add a caption.

You cannot use this method to add a caption to lists. If you build

a complex list with headings, you can put lists inside a table,

remove the borders, and then add a caption.

Tactic 19 Use Readable Line Lengths

The length of a line of text affects readability. The best line length depends on several elements, including font size, the size of the page, and the medium. According to Lohr, the general rule is that, if the type size is small, the line should be shorter.

Reading a very long line of text is tiring because readers need to remember what they already read. When lines are too short, readability may decrease because there are too many breaks in phrases.

James Hartley, professor of applied psychology at the University of Keele and the author of *Designing Instructional Text*, recommends common-sense guidelines based on your audience and the actual text. For example, we shouldn't break sentences in a way that repeatedly disrupts meaning.

James Craig, a usability expert and the co-author of *Designing with Type*, says an ideal line length is 45 to 75 characters, including spaces and punctuation. Some web design and usability experts are now using min-width and max-width attributes, and other methods, to add optimal line-length numbers in responsive web designs.

Figure 5.9 shows the same text passage in different line lengths.

Figure 5.9 Text passage at 67 characters wide (top), 54 characters wide (middle), and 30 characters wide (bottom), Times New Roman 12 point

You cannot use this method to add a caption to lists. If you
build a complex list with headings, you can put lists inside a
table, remove the borders, and then add a caption.

You cannot use this method to add a caption to
lists. If you build a complex list with headings, you
can put lists inside a table, remove the borders, and
then add a caption.

You cannot use this method
to add a caption to lists. If
you build a complex list with
headings, you can put lists
inside a table, remove the
borders, and then add a
caption.

Resource: Microsoft Word Count

If you want to count the number of characters in a line of text, you can use Microsoft Word. Select the line of text you want to count and then click the word count in the bottom left of the page (Figure 5.10). The Word Count dialog box will open. Find the "Characters (with spaces)" option. If you use other writing tools, search its Help section for "character count" to see if it offers this option.

Figure 5.10 Counting characters in a line of text in Microsoft Word (Windows)

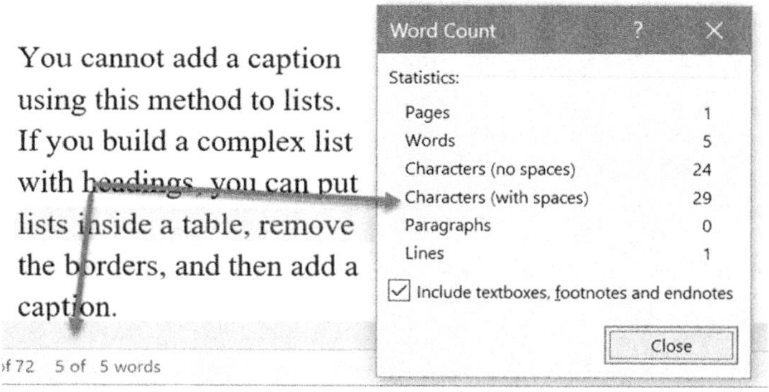

Tactic 20: Offer Adequate Contrast Between Text and Background

Earlier we discussed perception and its importance to learning. Contrast helps us perceive differences—and differences get attention.

Better contrast between text and background makes text easier to read. The best contrast is dark text on a very light background (Figure 5.11), according to Janice (Ginny) Reddish, an expert in information design and user experience research.

Figure 5.11 Dark text on a white background: excellent contrast (left). Dark text on a dark background: poor contrast (right).

You cannot use this method to add a caption to lists. If you build a complex list with headings, you can put lists inside a table, remove the borders, and then add a caption.	You cannot use this method to add a caption to lists. If you build a complex list with headings, you can put lists inside a table, remove the borders, and then add a caption.

When there is inadequate contrast, text is less legible. We should prefer high contrast for instructional text.

When we lay out pages, whether in print or in digital formats, contrast is one of the primary ways we help readers notice the most important things, such as the hierarchy of headings. Every component on the page is part of a message we are trying to send to people who are reading, watching, or listening. If we clutter up pages with too much content or too little contrast, it will be difficult for people to find the signal in the noise. In instructional content, especially, the signal must be clear, as memory has limited capacity.

If you search online for "contrast checkers," you will find tools that can check whether there is enough contrast. Next, I offer suggestions for practice. Practicing is how we learn, apply, and remember the tactics.

Don't forget you can practice these tactics any time you write or organize instruction. Go to the checklist at the end of the book and analyze which tactics are most needed. Then use the information in the book until you can teach the tactics to others!

Try It

We have reached the end of the tactics for **Strategy 3, Make Text Readable and Legible.** Select instruction you want to or someone has asked you to build. Then use the tactics in this chapter (recapped below) to make the content more learnable.

Tactic 13	**Test Readability** Use readability statistics in MS Word or elsewhere to evaluate readability/learnability.
Tactic 14	**Use Readable Fonts** Do you use only one or two fonts? Have you avoided overusing emphasis (UPPERCASE, **bold**, or *italics*)?
Tactic 15	**Use Readable Type Sizes** Is your type size readable at the distance viewers read it? Could audiences benefit from being able to change the size of the body text?
Tactic 16	**Left-Align Body Text** Is the text left-aligned?
Tactic 17	**Use Adequate White Space** Is there enough white space that the content doesn't look dense? Are the headings obvious? If you think more white space could be helpful, add it to see how it looks.
Tactic 18	**Space Lines of Text for Easy Reading** If the lines of text are too close or too far apart, change the spacing to make text easier to read.
Tactic 19	**Use Readable Line Lengths** Is the line length readable on all devices on which people will view your content?
Tactic 20	**Offer Adequate Contrast Between Text and Background** Make sure there is enough contrast between the text and background so everyone can easily read the text.

Do you need to get opinions from your users about how legible your text is? (Yes!)

Consider doing this exercise with a group of people so you can discuss the following with others.

- What was helpful, less helpful?
- What did you learn?
- Which parts of this exercise will you continue to use in the future?

CHAPTER 6

Strategy 4: Organize for Memory and Use

Usability designers (who enhance the ease of use of human-made systems and objects) make learnability a priority. Let's examine why usability experts care so much about learnability. If they care, we should too.

Question: When you are doing challenging work, you are ______ % interested in getting the work done and _______ % interested in learning how to do the work. (Fill in the two blanks so they add up to 100%.)

Answer: People like feeling smart. However, they don't necessarily love learning the things that help them feel smart, even though they may accept that this is part of the job. But they need to get from point A (what they need to learn) to point B (knowing what to do) quickly and with as little hassle as possible.

We must do the same thing when we design instruction. I discussed understanding your participants' needs in Strategy 1. If we don't understand their needs, anything we design is likely to miss the mark. If it misses the mark by a wide margin, we are wasting everyone's time and little or no learning occurs.

In this last strategy of the book, I discuss how to design instruction that meets audience needs by helping them know what the instruction will do for them, showing them where they will find what they need, and pointing them toward valuable job-oriented content.

You know how you look at the table of contents and skim a nonfiction book before buying it to see if it has the things you want to know? You're deciding whether the book and you have the same goals. The tactics in this strategy do similar things for instruction.

Figure 6.1 lists tactics that help us design for memory and use. We will talk about them in Tactics 21 through 28.

Figure 6.1 Tactics that help us organize for memory and use

Tactic 21: Connect to What People Already Know
Tactic 22: Design for Scanning
Tactic 23: Write Clear, Reader-friendly Objectives
Tactic 24: Tell People Where They Are Going
Tactic 25: Use Signals
Tactic 26: Make Content Job-ready
Tactic 27: Write Helpful Headings and Sub-headings
Tactic 28: Move Less-essential Content to Non-prime Space

Tactic 21 Connect to What People Already Know

In Chapter 2, I discussed how what people already know (prior knowledge) forms the foundation for additional learning. This has many implications. When organizing for memory and use, it means we should actively help people make critical connections between what they are learning and what they know.

There are many ways to help people connect something new to what they already know. One is to review what they've learned previously so they can remember what they *do* know. For example, if they are learning about changes to a policy, they often need to first review the existing policy, because they may not remember it. This helps them recognize the differences between the old and new policies. It also helps correct misunderstandings. "Our old policy covered people after 180 days. I had forgotten that." Correcting misunderstandings is essential because building upon a faulty foundation leads to faulty understanding and an inability to apply learning as intended.

Another way to help people connect what they are learning to what they already know is to know enough about your audience that you can build content that meets their specific needs. Knowing the prior knowledge of your audience helps you offer the right information and practice. That way, you do not assume they know more than they do, and you do not waste the time of people who already know what you are teaching.

Many teaching strategies depend specifically on prior knowledge. There are wide differences between how to train novices and how to train experts. (We call this the *expertise reversal effect,* and researchers are still studying the effect to see where and how it applies.)

What we do know is this: What we know is a foundation for everything we learn, so when we teach or design learning materials, it's critical that we:

- Make sure the foundation is accurate.
- Correct misconceptions.
- Connect new information to what is already known.

In other words, we need to ensure that people have accurate schemas. And we can do this through questions, practice, and real-life examples and scenarios.

For example, a course that trains people to analyze paint in older homes for potential health problems (including lead-based paint) might assume they already know how to find and analyze the level and state of paint deterioration.

This knowledge is a foundation for evaluating problems, knowing when repairs are critical, and knowing when you must use very specific work practices to remove paint.

If we assume people know this foundational information and it isn't part of the course, those who don't know it may have difficulty understanding the content and may make important mistakes. If people have inaccurate or inadequate understanding, they too may make mistakes.

A lot of training neglects to take the time to make sure participant schemas are correct; but, when we don't ask questions, check understanding, and fix misconceptions, we set people up for failure. One mark of an expert is well-developed and accurate schemas they can use to solve thorny problems.

When you are training people who are just learning a topic, they have little prior knowledge, and you may need to connect what they are learning to what they know by using analogies or stories they can relate to. You may also need to help people gain needed foundational knowledge so that what you are teaching makes sense.

For example, if you are training people how to give feedback, you can ask for examples of what works and doesn't work when giving feedback to a friend or spouse. Someone might offer that talking about your own reaction feels less critical than "You never..." statements. Another might say that piling on all the things that bother you is a tactic that will fail. Then you can discuss how this applies to workplace feedback.

People with more knowledge will have stories and insights you can use in training. For example, you might ask, "Can anyone discuss a situation where they didn't get adequate feedback?" You can use the answers to discuss outcomes and lessons learned.

Tactic 22: Design for Scanning

Many adults scan materials and web pages to evaluate whether the materials will meet their needs before committing to the time it takes to read them. Readers on the web, especially, scan and decide quickly whether the page or site is worth their time. We can make our materials better for this purpose by making instruction easy to scan. This not only helps people decide whether the content is likely to be useful, it helps them find content that specifically meets their job needs—now and later.

You may think that, if you lock your content inside online learning templates, this issue won't affect you. But most adults feel strongly about making choices, so not being able to decide whether your content will meet their needs may negatively affect how they feel about the content. For example, the lack of a useful menu on the right side of the course shown in Figure 6.2 may cause some people to decide it's poorly designed or likely not for them—even before they view a single page. Figure 6.3 shows the same course with a clearer menu.

Figure 6.2 Course menu does not show the course topics.

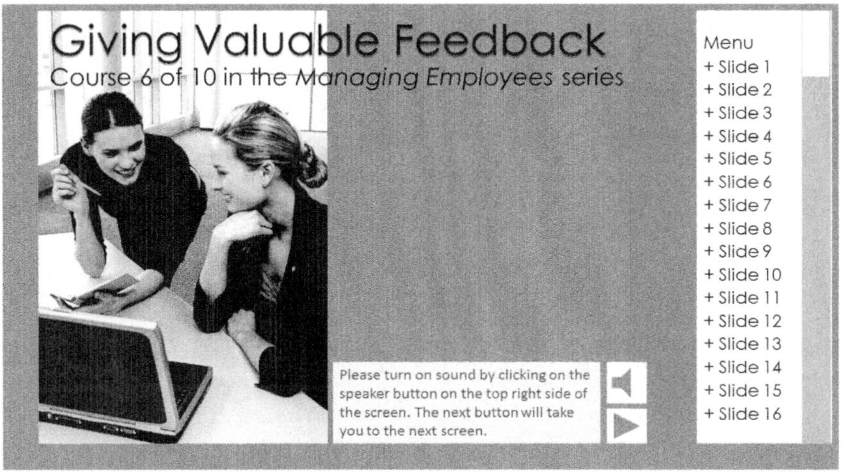

Figure 6.3 Course menu shows the course topics.

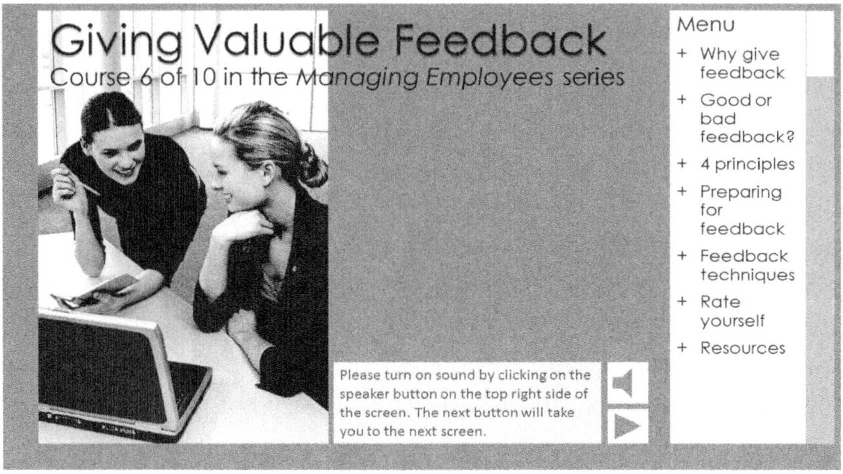

Here are the most important things we can do to help readers scan.

- Use meaningful headings and sub-headings (with words readers know and expect).
- Use ordered (numbered) and unordered (bulleted) lists and tables for collections of information.
- Add captions to concisely explain what the list, figure, or table shows.
- Add signals.

We'll discuss lists, tables, and captions in this tactic, and headings, subheadings, and signals in two other tactics.

Lists and Tables

Lists make scanning easier, and they are easier to read and find details in than paragraphs. They also improve understanding of arrangement and sequence (numbered lists). Lists often use less text than a paragraph and naturally add white space. I show list best practices in Table 6.1.

Table 6.1 How to make lists more understandable

Types of lists
• Use *numbered* (ordered) lists when the items have a natural order or hierarchy of importance. Clarify the order if it isn't obvious. • Use *bulleted* (unordered) lists when the items have no natural order or hierarchy of importance.
If the list is long
• Consider highlighting key words to improve scanning. • Don't overdo highlighting, as it makes reading more difficult. • Consider grouping list items into subgroups with sub-headings.
All lists
• Use parallel structure to start each list item. • When possible, sort lists logically: priority, date, person, department, task, cost, and so on. If we need to explain sorting, explain it as a heading.

"Parallel structure" means consistently using the same word structure. This makes lists easier to read and understand. In Figure 6.4, I highlighted the non-parallel word.

Figure 6.4 Parallel vs. non-parallel structure

Parallel:

There are three reasons it's important to give feedback.

Valuable feedback

- Helps staff understand expectations
- Develops your ability to ask for and manage input
- Builds positive relationships

Non-parallel:

There are three reasons it's important to give feedback.

Valuable feedback

- Helps staff understand expectations
- Developing your ability to ask for and manage input
- Builds positive relationships

Well-designed tables show relationships between items that readers could easily miss in a description. Clear row or column headers make these relationships clear, so it's critical to use clear, reader-friendly language in headers.

For example, Table 6.2 shows the relationship between different hardwood lumber grades and their sizes. Below the table is a partial example of the same text in paragraph format so you can judge the difference in the formats' ease of understanding.

Table 6.2 Standard hardwood lumber grades and sizes in a table (top) and paragraph (bottom)

Grade	Trade Name	Min width	Min length
Firsts and Seconds	FAS	6"	8'
Select	SEL	4"	6'
#1 Common	1C	3"	4'
#2A Common	2C	3"	4'
#2B Common	3AC	3"	4'
#3A Common	3BC	3"	4'

One way to summarize standard hardwood lumber grades is by trade name and minimum width and length. The highest grade is firsts and seconds, trade name FAS, with a minimum width of 6 inches and a minimum length of 8 feet. The next grade down is Select, and its trade name is SEL. It has a minimum width of 4 inches and a minimum length of 6 feet. Next is…

Research shows that, when the caption is clear, we can often leave out redundant description text. This is especially true when the meaning of the list, figure, or table is clear or when people are more experienced with the content.

Resource: Microsoft Word Insert Caption

Figure 6.5 shows adding a caption in a later version of Word. In Windows, you can right-click and select Insert Caption. Select Figure (for images) or Table (for tables), and then type the desired caption text.

Figure 6.5 Adding a caption in MS Word (Windows)

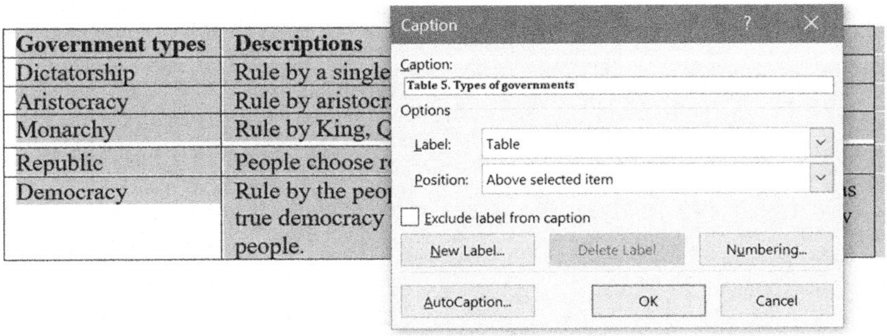

You cannot add a caption to bulleted and numbered lists. But you can put lists inside a one-cell table, remove the borders, and then add a caption, if desired. I do this regularly. I also use two columns and two rows for side-by-side lists. To remove the border, click on the table and select No Border from the Borders item on the Design tab (Windows). I show removing the border from a table in Figure 6.6.

Figure 6.6 Select No Border to remove the border from a table.

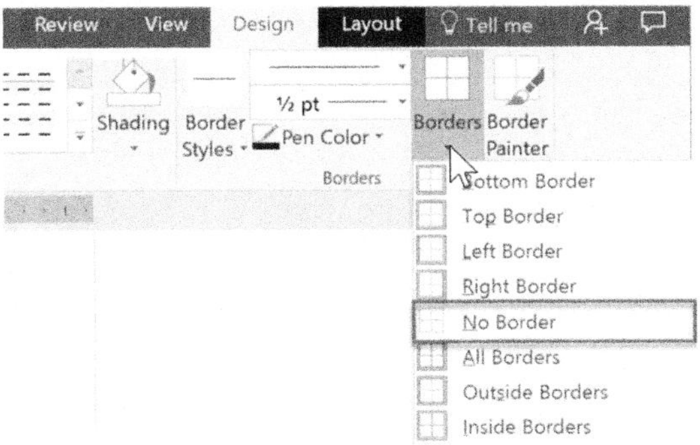

Tactic 23: Write Clear, Reader-Friendly Objectives

When we develop organizational instruction, one of the first things we must do is decide what to include. And there is a ready but not very satisfying (to many people) answer to what you *should* include: only what people need for what they need to be able to do. No more, no less.

Without well-written learning objectives, created before we begin to write any content, we are taking a stab in the dark about what to include and how to train. Because of the memory constraints I discussed in Chapter 2, we know that adding too much content makes it harder to learn.

I often hear discussions at learning-oriented conferences about why we *don't* need to give learning objectives to participants. It is *the opposite* of what research tells us to do.

What research tells us is that supplying learning objectives promotes learning. Clear and accurate learning objectives tell people the goals of instruction and what we expect them to do. This encourages meeting those objectives.

Learning objectives should specifically state what people should be able to do because of the instruction. We commonly help people learn two types of knowledge: declarative and procedural. Table 6.3 explains how they are different.

Table 6.3 Types of learnable knowledge

Declarative	• Facts and concepts, things that can be "declared" • Know "what and why" **Examples:** How this type of copy machine works, rapid transit systems routes in [city], the federal laws that apply to interviewing, lawful and unlawful interview questions, how content clarity improves readability
Procedural	• Application and problem solving in the real world, such as the tasks they must perform • Know "when and how" **Examples:** Find and fix the faulty parts, get to work and home using rapid transit, perform a lawful interview when interviewee shares personal information, write clear content using the seven tactics

It is far too common for us to teach only declarative knowledge and spend little or no time on procedural knowledge. Table 6.4 shows activities I might use for both types of knowledge when I teach how to write for content clarity in a classroom workshop.

Table 6.4 Activities for declarative and procedural knowledge for a single training topic (and its associated objectives)

Topic: Writing for content clarity	
Learning objectives: • Define clarity. • List at least two reasons clarity is critical to instructional content. • Apply seven specific tactics to make instructional content more clear. • Select tactics needed to clarify specific instructional content.	
Declarative	1. Define clarity. 2. Explain why clarity is important to instructional content.
Procedural	1. Apply each tactic to pre-selected content. 2. Do a rewrite of two pieces of instructional content using the clarity tactics (asynchronous, synchronous, group exercise). 3. Share your rewrite and get feedback. 3.1. How well did you apply the tactics? 3.2. What would you (the person giving feedback) have done differently? 4. Review clarity tactics.

Declarative knowledge helps us understand procedural knowledge. We see instances of where people can perform (procedural knowledge), but they don't understand why (declarative knowledge). An example of this is where customer service reps are using scripts to answer customer questions but don't have enough understanding to go "off script." Deep learning means the rep knows why and can apply what he or she knows in various situations. If the caller says, "But I wasn't online when this happened," the rep has enough understanding of this issue to go in different directions based on the new information. This is why I asked you to put the concepts in Chapter 2 into your own words. (Self-explanations are one such deep learning strategy.)

When we don't supply learning objectives or they are unclear, people don't know what we expect them to know and do. And, if we write them at a low level ("List the three different scenarios...") when people really need to do something more complex ("Compute benefits under the three different scenarios..."), we are doing people a disservice.

Tactic 24: Tell People Where They Are Going

One of the reasons people like navigation systems in their cars and navigation apps on their smartphones is that they help our brains with a complex aspect of daily living. Driving itself is complex, and trying to use maps while driving can be dangerous. (Do any of you remember buying map books and reviewing your route before going somewhere? Or buying AAA map books when traveling?)

Likewise, it can help cognition when we supply what we call an *advance organizer,* which shows where we are going. There are two primary types of advance organizers:

- Introduction to the topic
- Planner

Introduction to the Topic

This type of advance organizer gives an overview of the topic and connects the topic to what participants already know. In Chapter 2, we discussed how prior knowledge helps people learn and helps learning stick.

In this type of advance organizer, we should show how we organize the topic. A good way to do this is with an outline at the beginning of the topic, and headings and sub-headings that match the outline exactly, as shown in Figure 6.7.

Figure 6.7 Matching outline and headings/subheadings

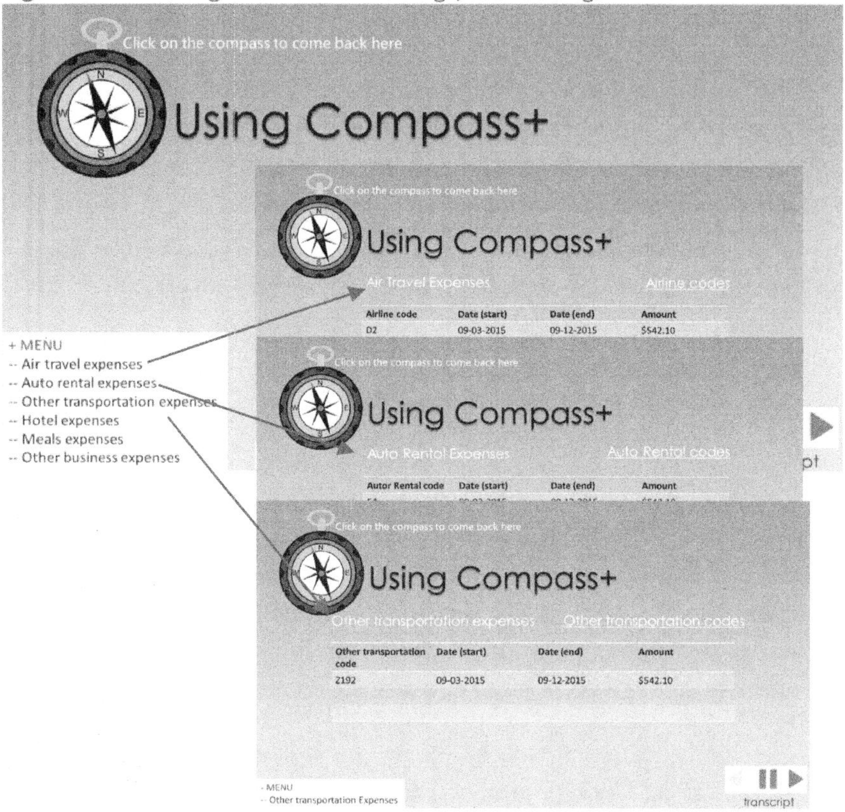

Figure6.7 shows the menu as an advanced organizer for the travel expense program training. Each menu item is the heading for the part of the training that shows how to use that part of the program.

I used an advance organizer for each strategy in the book. The table of contents serves as an overall advance organizer. I tried very hard to use terms in the headings and sub-headings that would be understandable to people who don't already know this material. For example, instead of calling this tactic "Use Advance Organizers," I called it "Tell People Where They Are Going." You can let me know if my advance organizers were helpful and I will gladly update them if needed.

Planner

An advance organizer can also be a planner, which helps people know what we expect them to complete, as well as the due dates, the steps they need to take, examples of desired outcomes, and so on.

Examples of this type of advance organizer include:

- Syllabus
- Task checklists
- Examples
- Job aids with task sequence

The main purpose for offering these types of aids is to ease memory and retrieval of memory. Too many trainers and instructors think that, once they have verbally discussed something with participants, those participants know what we expect and what to do. As discussed in Chapter 2, working memory can deal with only a few chunks of information at a time. If people are new to the information and we are repeatedly giving them new information, they will not be able to handle all of it. We need to offer memory aids.

In many learning situations—formal (courses) or informal (talk between people about how to do something)—we expect people to remember what we show or tell. But that expectation is absurd. Given everything people have read and listen to, we should expect them to forget—and we should provide support for remembering.

For each strategy, I show a list of the tactics that go along with it. At the end of the book, I supply a job aid/checklist of the strategies and tactics, with concise recommendations distilled from the book. I include these items to show you where we are going, help you see how I organize these evidence-based suggestions, assist you with remembering the strategies and tactics, and help you remember to apply them when working on a project.

Tactic 25: Use Signals

Signals are a way to send information through gestures, actions, or sounds. Did you see *The Hunger Games*? Do you remember when Rue used the Mockingjay whistle? She was signaling to the others on her team.

Signals, as applied to the text and organization of instructional content, tell people how the content is organized (and how people should organize it in their minds) and what is most important. Working memory is a precious and limited commodity, and people cannot pay attention to and process everything we want to give them. We can use signals to clearly point out what is most important.

There are many types of signals, but I will limit our discussion to the ones we (should) use regularly (Table 6.5).

Table 6.5. Types of signals and their purpose

Signal Type	**Purpose**
Advance organizer	How to organize the topic/domain
Headings, sub-headings	How to organize the topic/domain, should match the table of contents
Categorization	How to organize the topic Sequential (step 1, step 2...), time-based (first, second...), rules, tasks, spatial (front to back), and so on
Bold, italics, callouts	What is most important; *don't overuse*
Ordered (numbered) list	In order of importance (hierarchy)

I discussed advance organizers in Tactic 24. They can be text, graphic (like mine), or media based. Let's imagine this book was, instead, in an online format and—when you came to the advance organizer for Strategy 1: Understand Your Audience's Needs—the following advance organizer appeared (Figure 6.8).

Figure 6.8 Possible advance organizer for Patti Shank's *Write and Organize for Deeper Learning* course

Instructions: Please click on each of the numbers below to find out more about the four tactics you will use to better understand your audience's needs.

Question: Based on everything you have read in this book, is the advance organizer in Figure 6.8 good, bad, or neither?

Answer: My answer? It's probably not the best way to show the tactics for Strategy 1. Here are two problems. Some people will skip it because it takes more time to read and digest than my simple advance organizer. And there is one more huuuuge minus: You cannot see the four tactics at the same time, which reduces the usefulness of the advance organizer for understanding (and remembering) the organization of the topic. Boo.

Designers and developers have limited time, too. To build the activity in Figure 6.8 takes more time than it took to build my advance organizer.

Because a simpler advance organizer is easier to build and is more likely to be used (in this case), it's a better use of our time. It'd be better for designers to spend their time making their materials more learnable rather than adding bells and whistles that probably don't help, and may hinder, learning.

Tactic 26: Make Content Job-Ready

Some of the content we develop for instruction is likely to be extremely useful back on the job. How do we decide what pieces might be useful on the job? And what do we do to make those pieces ready?

One thing we know is that, when people are doing their jobs, they're unlikely to dig back through course materials to find the tables, lists, and other information they would find helpful as support materials. It's one of the primary reasons I wrote this as a book.

To make content job-ready, we need to

1. Decide which parts of the training materials are likely to be useful on the job.
2. Put those elements in a format ready for job usage.
3. Use these materials in training just as they will be used on the job so participants learn how to use them and get used to using them.

Here's a real example from a real project. During the analysis phase, we determined that training for a complex system should consist primarily of many short example videos that got progressively more complex. Each video lesson supplied a short job aid that specified the steps used for doing those tasks. Participants used the job aid in a learning activity in which they did tasks similar to the ones in the video.

Using the job aid triggered their memory of what they saw in the video and supported their memory when they did the task themselves. And it would be available to use when they did those tasks in the future.

Decide which training materials are likely to be useful on the job

To know which parts of the training materials will be useful after training, you must understand how the training intersects with job tasks. For example, if you are training retail staff to use a new cash register, the list of codes for each type of sale will be useful as a job aid at the register. Likewise, a job aid with the basic steps to follow to ring up a sale and take returns will likely be useful.

You don't want to hand people 83 job aids that cover all training tasks. Ask yourself this question: What am I training people on that either needs initial memory support (when they go to do it on the job) or will need ongoing memory support (because they will do it rarely, it's too complex, or it has too many details to memorize)? Those are likely candidates for needing to be job-ready and not just training-ready.

Table 6.6 shows items taught in training that may need initial memory support and ongoing memory support for a course on reimbursement for business travel. Depending on how often a person travels, all might be candidates for ongoing support.

Table 6.6 Memory support items for business travel course

Things possibly needing initial memory support	**Things possibly needing ongoing memory support**
• The four steps for getting expenses reimbursed • Allowed and disallowed expenses • The hotels with which the company has discounts	• The codes to enter for the different hotel chains and airlines • The sites, names, and phone numbers of who to contact if you have problems with reimbursement

For example, Figure 6.9 shows a slide from a narrated slideshow that tells employees how to do business travel expense reports. This slide discusses allowed and disallowed travel expenses. Look at the top of the slide. You will see two links:

1. An in-depth job aid with a full list of items that are allowable and not allowable, with more in-depth notes
2. The company's full expense policy

Figure 6.9 Slide from narrated slideshow with links to job aid and expense policy

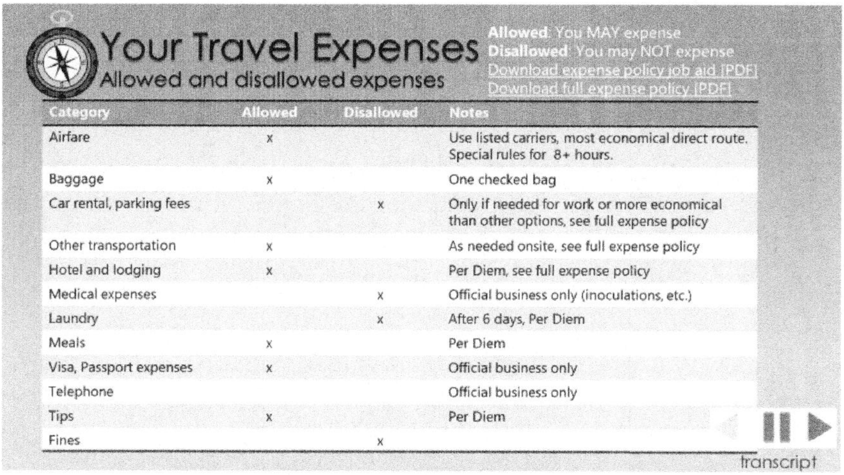

Category	Allowed	Disallowed	Notes
Airfare	x		Use listed carriers, most economical direct route. Special rules for 8+ hours.
Baggage	x		One checked bag
Car rental, parking fees		x	Only if needed for work or more economical than other options, see full expense policy
Other transportation	x		As needed onsite, see full expense policy
Hotel and lodging	x		Per Diem, see full expense policy
Medical expenses		x	Official business only (inoculations, etc.)
Laundry		x	After 6 days, Per Diem
Meals	x		Per Diem
Visa, Passport expenses	x		Official business only
Telephone			Official business only
Tips	x		Per Diem
Fines		x	

The narrator discussed how to use this job-ready content. And, in the next section, on how to use the online travel system, she reminds people they can use the job aid when doing the practice exercises.

All the job-ready content is also available from links in the Downloads section of the course. This makes it easy for people who want this content to find what they need without having to go through the pages of the course. No one wants to do that!

Some people have told me they think that adding memory support sounds like too much work. If you think so, remember that designing in the ways I discuss in this book *saves* work because you spend more time on things that truly make a difference and less on things that don't make a difference. In any event, doing the things that help people learn is what good instruction is all about. When we don't do them, our work is far less valuable.

I've never heard a carpenter complain that measuring more than once to verify that his or her measurements are accurate takes too much time. It saves time from having to do it over or having to find carpenters who make fewer mistakes.

Put those elements in a format ready for job usage

Once you've figured out which elements from training will best support memory, you want to decide what format you should put them it. Again, you will want to find out what format will be best for workers. PDFs? Laminated cards? Files?

Watch people work, ask questions, and figure out what will be best *for them*. Consider how often you will need to update them, too. If the process changes often, you may have different needs than if the process never changes.

In many of my projects, we use downloadable PDFs. But, on a few of my projects, clients didn't want people to be able to give the PDFs to others, so we put restraints on printing and copying. If someone has the right programs, however, they can copy, print, and send pretty much everything.

Use these materials in training just as they will be used on the job

To help people get used to using the job aids and other materials that are in ready-for-job-use format, you will want participants to use them in training. The best way to do this is to create training activities in which participants use these elements as memory support. Table 6.7 shows examples of training activities in which participants use the job aid to answer the questions or perform a training scenario. These activities train them to use the job aid to file an accurate expense report.

Table 6.7 Memory support job aid and training activities for business travel course

Memory support job aid	Training activities
• The four steps for getting expenses reimbursed • Allowed and disallowed expenses • The hotels with which the company has discounts • The codes to enter for the different hotel chains and airlines • The sites, names, and phone numbers of who to contact if you have problems with reimbursement	• Put the steps in the right order • Questions: Is this expense allowed? • Scenario 1: File this expense report • Scenario 2: File this expense report • Scenario 3: File this expense report

Tactic 27: Write Helpful Headings and Sub-headings

Headings and sub-headings are key ways readers scan content and figure out its organization—and are some of the strongest cues we offer about content organization and structure.

For example, if you look at the table of contents in this book, you can see which tactics belong to each strategy. I intentionally used lower-level headings for tactics under each higher-level strategy so you would visually notice which tactics belonged to which strategy.

For headings and sub-headings to show organization and structure and help people find what they need in instructional and support information, we need to do two things:

- Describe the content in reader-friendly language
- Use the correct heading level

Describe the content in reader-friendly language

Consider headings introductions to the content below. Headings need to tell people what they will be reading—and they should offer information that helps people scan for the information they want to find (especially when they are using the content for support).

Headings also need to be in reader-friendly language so people understand what the heading means. Each heading must also be different from other headings so people can tell what's different about that section of content versus another section of content. Figure 6.10 shows two versions of headings and sub-headings for an online data privacy course.

Figure 6.10 Good and not-so-good headings and sub-headings for a course on keeping your online data private

Good headings and sub-headings	**Not-so-good headings and sub-headings**
1. Is your online data private?	1. I ain't got no (privacy)
1.1. How is your data tracked?	1.1. Nowhere to hide
1.2. What is collected?	1.2. We gotcha
1.3. How is it used?	1.3. See how!
1.4. Check your online footprint	2. It's happening (to you)
2. Evaluate online services	2.1. Who are these folks?
2.1. Who owns this site?	2.2. Betcha didn't read this
2.2. How to evaluate the terms of service	3. Hiding while
3. Keep your data private	3.1. Browsing
3.1. Browser settings	3.2. Searching
3.2. Search	3.3. Chatting
3.3. Chat	3.4. Emailing
3.4. Email	4. Your turn
4. Resources	

The headings and sub-headings on the left in Figure 6.10 are descriptive and clear. Each topic's heading clearly describes what you can expect to learn in that topic. The sub-headings clearly belong with the topic.

On the right, the headings and sub-headings are funny, but they don't describe the content. You might enjoy the quips, but you may have to hunt to find what you need.

Use the correct heading level

If you look at the table of contents for this book—or the left outline in Figure 6.10—you'll notice that the sub-headings are subordinate to headings. That means certain subtopics fall within that topic.

By using different levels of headings, I am showing you which subtopics fall within a given topic. The rationale for being very clear about the level of my topics is to help you see how I organized the content in my book. I want you to notice certain things.

1. I offered four strategies to help you write and organize for deeper learning:
    - Analyze your audience's needs
    - Write for clarity
    - Make text readable and legible
    - Organize for memory and use
2. Each strategy has several specific tactics you can use to carry out that strategy. Each tactic belongs to one of the four strategies. Thus, I used a lower-level heading to point out that it is part of that strategy.

The headings and sub-headings in the left column of Figure 6.10 work similarly. There are four topics. Most of the topics have sub-topics, which are subordinate to the topic. Figure 6.11 shows the menu of the course, opened in the lower left of the home screen.

You can also see how the sub-topics are subordinate to the main topics, as the topics are bold and the sub-topics are indented and not bold.

Figure 6.11 Headings and sub-headings in the menu of an online privacy course

Tactic 28: Move Less-Essential Content to Non-Prime Space

There is limited space in learning content, especially on digital screens. Cramming content onto a screen often looks bad, makes it hard to find what's most important, and can reduce readability and legibility, as we learned in the tactics in Strategy 3.

Yet there's usually a need to include *some* less-essential content because that material may be useful for questions specific audience members have. Also, to be practical, you may have to include some content you don't want to include. This isn't a license to add a bunch of extra content. If you do, even if it's in non-prime space, it will make your materials look junked-up and hard to digest.

One good approach, when less-essential content must be included, is to move it to non-prime space such as glossaries, appendixes, downloadable documents, links, or other supplementary spots.

Here are some dos and don'ts for moving less-essential content.

DO	DON'T
✓ Decide which type of non-prime space (glossary, appendixes, downloadable documents, links, other) makes the most sense based on frequency and type of use.	× Don't keep "nice to know" content, especially for less-expert audiences. Overwhelming memory is a real possibility.
✓ Be consistent. Use the same type of non-prime space for the same type of content. For example, definitions are in glossaries, documents are in a resource section, etc.	× Don't provide a long list of links—especially for people who are new to the topic. Curate them to the very best ones.
✓ Make sure that moving the	× Don't use this tactic as an

DO	DON'T
content doesn't create any confusion or gaps.	excuse to add non-valuable content. Ask yourself, "Who needs this?"
✓ When using links, create a maintenance schedule for checking that links work.	

In Figure 6.12, you can see that certain content is in non-prime space, under the topic Resources.

Figure 6.12 Non-prime space (Resources) used for resources and a message from the company

People are less likely to read content you move to non-prime space. Be sure there are no ramifications, legal or otherwise, for having this content "out of the way."

Try It

We have reached the end of the tactics for **Strategy 4, Organize for Memory and Use.** Select instruction you want to or someone has asked you to build. Then use the tactics in this chapter (recapped below) to make the content more learnable.

Tactic 21	**Connect to What People Already Know** Teach to what people already know as it is the foundation of what they are able to learn.
Tactic 22	**Design for Scanning** Turn lists of items in body text into lists, either numbered (ordered) or bulleted (unordered). Present the lists in a logical order when there is a logical order: priority, date, person/department, task, cost, and so on. Use tables that show relationships. Use clear, reader-friendly row or column headers to make the relationships clear to the reader. Using captions on lists, figures, and tables to concisely and clearly describe what you are showing. Let captions stand in for text descriptions when captions offer enough explanation.
Tactic 23	**Write Clear, Reader-Friendly Objectives** Tell people the declarative and procedural knowledge they will gain from training. You are setting expectations and goals for training.
Tactic 24	**Tell People Where They Are Going** Use **advance organizers** to show how the topic should be organized. You should also introduce the topic and tie it to what participants already know.
Tactic 25	Use **signals** to show how the topic is organized and what is most important.

	• Advance organizers, headings and sub-headings, and categorization show how to organize the topics. Make sure to use reader-friendly language. • Use bold, italics, and callouts to point out the most important information, but don't overuse them. • When building lists, number ordered list items in order of importance, as numbered lists convey an order. If there is no order, use bulleted lists.
Tactic 26	**Make Content Job-Ready** Make content job-ready by finding out which content will be useful on the job as well as in training—then provide this content in a format people can easily use on the job.
Tactic 27	**Write Helpful Headings and Sub-Headings** Use headings and sub-headings that describe the content in reader-friendly language, show how topics are organized, and show which topics are subordinate to main topics.
Tactic 28	**Move Less-Essential Content to Non-Prime Space** Move content not everyone needs to non-prime space to make it easier for participants to find and concentrate on the most critical instructional messages.

Consider doing this exercise with a group of people so you can discuss the following with others.

- What was helpful, less helpful?
- What did you learn?
- Which parts of this exercise will you continue to use in the future?

CHAPTER 7

Now What?

This chapter contains four tools to help you use the strategies and tactics in this book.

- A **retrieval practice activity** to help you remember the strategies and tactics in this book. I know it will be easier for you to use the tactics if you don't have to continually refer to the book.
- A **checklist** (job aid) of all the strategies and tactics and the main tasks that correspond with each tactic. It's hard (but not impossible—especially if you use the retrieval practice activity) to remember 28 tactics, but the checklist will help you remember them and what they mean. Feel free to annotate them with your own notes and insights from the book.
- Special **offer** on a writing tool.
- A list of **references**—the research and other references that support the strategies and tactics.

I'd be grateful if you could tell me what you think of this book. For example:

- Was the book valuable to you? Why or why not? Was it worth what you paid? What would you change? Would you buy more of these how-to books based on research? Here are topics I am considering writing for this series.
  a) Using Questions and Examples for Deeper Learning
  b) Build More Learnable Multimedia
  c) Create Job Aids and Performance Support
  d) Assess Learning and Performance
  e) Evaluate and Revise Instruction
  f) Building Interaction for Deeper Learning

You can reach out by going to my website (www.pattishank.com) and finding the contact form near the bottom.

I use what you tell me to revise and fine-tune what I write. I get super excited when readers write to me. It often makes my day! And I'm especially grateful there are other learning geeks who want to make a real difference in their organizations and elsewhere. Yay!!!

Thank YOU.

Retrieval Practice

Retrieval practice is a powerful learning activity for improving recall of specific information. It's simple and it's another tactic you can adopt. Primarily, it involves retrieving information from long-term memory. Each time we retrieve the same information, we strengthen our memory for that information.

Try to list the tactics without looking through the book. Check your answers against the table of contents, Table 2.2, or the checklist that follows. Then correct your answers and practice memorizing the right answers for five minutes. Try again in a few days. Keep doing this at slightly longer intervals.

Date: Try 1

Strategies	**What are the tactics for each strategy?**
Strategy 1: Understand your audience's needs (Tactics 1–4)	
Strategy 2: Write for clarity (Tactics 5–12)	

Strategy 3: Make text readable and legible (Tactics 13–20)	
Strategy 4: Organize for memory and use (Tactics 21–28)	

How many did you get right?   /28

Date: Try 2

Strategies	**What are the tactics for each strategy?**
Strategy 1: Understand your audience's needs (Tactics 1–4)	
Strategy 2: Write for clarity (Tactics 5–12)	
Strategy 3: Make text readable and legible (Tactics 13–20)	

Strategy 4: Organize for memory and use (Tactics 21–28)	

How many did you get right? /28

Date: Try 3

Strategies	**What are the tactics for each strategy?**
Strategy 1: Understand your audience's needs (Tactics 1–4)	
Strategy 2: Write for clarity (Tactics 5–12)	
Strategy 3: Make text readable and legible (Tactics 13–20)	

Strategy 4: Organize for memory and use (Tactics 21–28)	

How many did you get right? /28

Date: Try 4

Strategies	**What are the tactics for each strategy?**
Strategy 1: Understand your audience's needs (Tactics 1–4)	
Strategy 2: Write for clarity (Tactics 5–12)	
Strategy 3: Make text readable and legible (Tactics 13–20)	

Strategy 4: Organize for memory and use (Tactics 21–28)	

How many did you get right?   /28

Write and Organize for Deeper Learning Checklist

Purpose: Use this job aid/checklist as a memory aid for the strategies and tactics. The descriptions to the right of the tactics are concise recommendations distilled from the book.

Strategy 1: Understand Your Audience's Needs

Tactic 1	**Analyze Your Audience's Needs** Find out how what you are teaching intersects with the work your audience members do. What tasks are they doing when they apply the knowledge and skills? What kinds of problems come up that make it hard to apply the knowledge and skills? What is hard to do and how can this training help them? What would make the training most valuable to their work?
Tactic 2	**Write for the Right Level of Prior Knowledge** How much do potential audience members know about what you are teaching or designing? What content isn't valuable to them because they already know it or because it doesn't help them with the important parts of their job? What misconceptions do they have that you need to fix?
Tactic 3	**Make the Purpose Obvious** How will you let audience members know right away how training information pertains to their needs? How will you write titles and training information so they know whether training and materials are relevant to their needs and goals?
Tactic 4	**Answer Audience Questions** What questions do potential audience members have about what you are teaching or designing?

Strategy 2: Write for Clarity

Tactic 5	**Determine Your Key Points** Start by determining the key points and writing to them. Or find the key points. Does the writing veer from them? If so, analyze which content to remove and which messages need to be more noticeable.
Tactic 6	**Use Shorter Sentences** Divide your longer sentences into shorter sentences.
Tactic 7	**Remove Less-Valuable Sentences** Look for sentences that don't add anything or repeat what you have already said and remove them.
Tactic 8	**Use Simpler, More Common Words and Phrases** Use the Plain Language Simple Words and Phrases list or Dr. Blank's Wordiness List to replace complex words and phrases with simpler words and phrases.
Tactic 9	**Talk Directly to Your Reader or Listener** Change wording to make it sound as if you are talking directly to the reader. Use *you* and *we*. Make your language more conversational and friendly.
Tactic 10	**Prefer Active Voice** Use active voice. Turn on Microsoft Word's passive sentences finder and search for passive sentences. Make them active.
Tactic 11	**Be Direct About What People Need to Do** Tell your reader what they need to do. Don't make them figure it out!
Tactic 12	**Make Long Descriptions Easier to Understand** Can any be more concise or replaced with a graphic?

Strategy 3: Make Text Readable and Legible

Tactic 13	**Test Readability** Use readability statistics in MS Word or elsewhere to evaluate readability/learnability.
Tactic 14	**Use Readable Fonts** Do you use only one or two fonts? Have you avoided overusing emphasis (UPPERCASE, **bold**, or *italics*)?
Tactic 15	**Use Readable Type Sizes** Is your type size readable at the distance viewers read it? Could audiences benefit from being able to change the size of the body text?
Tactic 16	**Left-Align Body Text** Is the text left-aligned?
Tactic 17	**Use Adequate White Space** Is there enough white space that the content doesn't look dense? Are the headings obvious? If you think more white space could be helpful, add it to see how it looks.
Tactic 18	**Space Lines of Text for Easy Reading** If the lines of text are too close or too far apart, change the spacing to make text easier to read.
Tactic 19	**Use Readable Line Lengths** Is the line length readable on all devices on which people will view your content?
Tactic 20	**Offer Adequate Contrast Between Text and Background** Make sure there is enough contrast between the text and background so everyone can easily read the text.

Do you need to get opinions from your users about how legible your text is? (Yes!)

Strategy 4: Organize for Memory and Use

Tactic 21	**Connect to What People Already Know** Teach to what people already know as it is the foundation of what they are able to learn.
Tactic 22	**Design for Scanning** Turn lists of items in body text into lists, either numbered (ordered) or bulleted (unordered). Present the lists in a logical order when there is a logical order: priority, date, person/department, task, cost, and so on. Use tables that show relationships. Use clear, reader-friendly row or column headers to make the relationships clear to the reader. Using captions on lists, figures, and tables to concisely and clearly describe what you are showing. Let captions stand in for text descriptions when captions offer enough explanation.
Tactic 23	**Write Clear, Reader-Friendly Objectives** Tell people the declarative and procedural knowledge they will gain from training. You are setting expectations and goals for training.
Tactic 24	**Tell People Where They Are Going** Use **advance organizers** to show how the topic should be organized. You should also introduce the topic and tie it to what participants already know.
Tactic 25	Use **signals** to show how the topic is organized and what is most important. • Advance organizers, headings and sub-headings, and categorization show how to organize the topics. Make sure to use reader-friendly language. • Use bold, italics, and callouts to point out the most important information, but don't overuse them.

	• When building lists, number ordered list items in order of importance, as numbered lists convey an order. If there is no order, use bulleted lists.
Tactic 26	**Make Content Job-Ready** Make content job-ready by finding out which content will be useful on the job as well as in training—then provide this content in a format people can easily use on the job.
Tactic 27	**Write Helpful Headings and Sub-Headings** Use headings and sub-headings that describe the content in reader-friendly language, show how topics are organized, and show which topics are subordinate to main topics.
Tactic 28	**Move Less-Essential Content to Non-Prime Space** Move content not everyone needs to non-prime space to make it easier for participants to find and concentrate on the most critical instructional messages.

Want More?

The Make It Learnable series shows you how to apply information and usability research, learning research, and writing research to your instructional projects. This is the first book in the series, and *Practice and Feedback for Deeper Learning* is now available as well and can be found on Amazon internationally.

To know when each book becomes available, sign up for email on my website (www.pattishank.com), follow me on Twitter (@pattishank), or check Amazon.

If you want to offer any Make It Learnable books to a team, I offer quantity discounts. I can train your team, group, or conference, and supply heavily discounted Make It Learnable books that are used in my training sessions. Contact me at patti@learningpeaks.com.

Thank you for helping me improve research-based practices in organizational and adult learning. My goal is to make it easier for *anyone* who writes learning content (including content experts, instructional designers, teachers, and instructors) to build learnable instruction. Just. That. Simple.

What Is the Readability of This Book?

The readability score of the text in this book, according to MS Word's Flesch Reading Ease, is 59.8.

Later versions of Microsoft Word (usually under Word Options) include readability statistics based on Flesch Reading Ease. This readability scale uses scores from 0 to 100. The higher the number, the easier the text is to read. I wanted readability to be in the 60–70 range because I didn't want readability to be an issue for *anyone*.

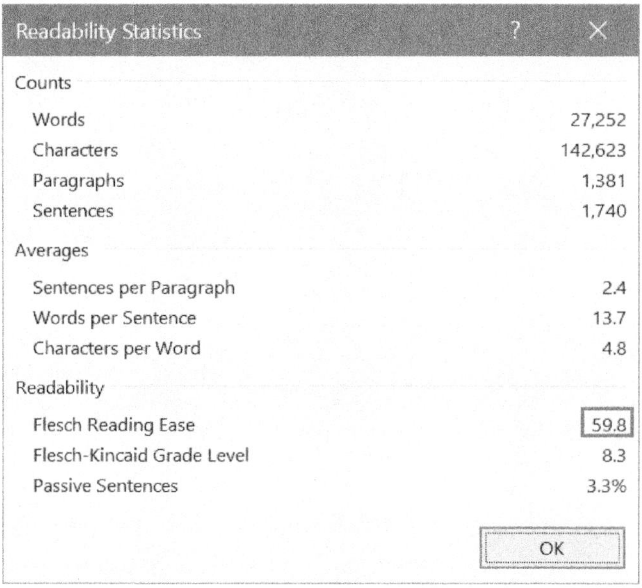

References

This reference list includes the primary references that support the insights and recommendations in this book. I categorized the links, but some could appear in more than one place. I recommend looking for books on eBay and half.com and other used book sites so you can find inexpensive used copies.

Many of the articles can be found online by searching for the article title. I am building an online database of freely available (online) research articles for our field so you can also check pattishank.com for URLs. This will make it easier for me to remove links if authors or publishers don't want their works freely found.

Adult Skills

OECD Skills Outlook https://www.oecd.org/skills/piaac

U.S. Department of Education, National Center for Education Statistics, 2003 National Assessment of Adult Literacy https://nces.ed.gov/naal

Learning

Bransford, J. D. (1979). *Human Cognition: Learning, Understanding, and Remembering*. Belmont, CA: Wadsworth.

Bloom, Benjamin S. (1968). Learning for mastery. UCLA - CSEIP - Evaluation Comment. 1.

Bransford, J.D., Brown, A.L. & Cocking, R.R. (Eds.). (2000). *How People Learn: Brain, Mind, Experience, and School: Expanded Edition*. Washington, DC: National Academy Press.

Clark, R. (2003). *Building expertise: Cognitive methods for training and performance improvement* (2nd ed.). Silver Spring, MD: International Society for Performance Improvement.

Flavell, J. H. (1979). Metacognition and cognitive monitoring: A new area of cognitive-developmental inquiry. American Psychologist, 34, 906–911.

Fogarty, R. (1994). *How to Teach for Metacognition*. Palatine, IL: IRI/Skylight Publishing.

Lee, H.W. Lim, K.Y., Grabowski, B.L. (2008). Generative learning: Principles and implications for making meaning. In J. M. Spector, M.D. Merrill, J. van Merrienboer, & M.P. Driscoll, (Eds.) *Handbook of Research on Educational Communications and Technology* (3rd ed.).

Mayer, R. E. (2009). *Multimedia Learning*. New York: Cambridge University Press.

Mayer, R. E., & Clark, R. C. C. (2010) Instructional strategies for receptive learning environments. In K. H. Silber & W. R. Foshay (Eds.), *Handbook of Improving Performance in the Workplace* (Vol. 1, pp. 298-328). Hoboken, NJ: John Wiley & Sons.

Mayer, R.E. (2014). *The Cambridge Handbook of Multimedia Learning* (2nd ed.). Cambridge, England: Cambridge University Press.

Stern, E. (2017). Individual differences in the learning potential of human beings. *npj Science of Learning*. 2(2). https://www.nature.com/articles/s41539-016-0003-0#Sec6

Learnability

Costabile, M. F., De Marsico M., Lanzilotti R., Plantsman, V. L., & Roselli, T. (2005). On the usability evaluation of e-learning applications. Proceedings of the 38th Hawaii International Conference on System Sciences.

Grossman, T., Fitzmaurice, G., and Attar, R. (2009). A survey of software learnability: metrics, methodologies and guidelines. In *Proceedings of the 27th international Conference on Human Factors in Computing Systems*. New York, NY, 649-658.

Guthrie, J. T. (1972). Learnability versus readability of texts. *The Journal of Educational Research, 65*(6).

Memory, Cognitive Load

Ausubel, D. P. (1968). *Educational Psychology: A Cognitive View*. New York: Holt, Rinehart & Winston.

Chen, B., & Hirumi, A. (2009). Effects of advance organizers on learning for differentiated learners in a fully Web-based course. International Journal of Instructional Technology & Distance Learning.

Clark, R. C., Nguyen, F., & Sweller, J. (2011). *Efficiency in Learning: Evidence-based Guidelines to Manage Cognitive Load.* San Francisco, CA: Pfeiffer.

Mayer, R. E., Heiser, J., & Lonn, S. (2001). Cognitive constraints on multimedia learning: When presenting more material results in less understanding. Journal of Educational Psychology, 93, 187-198.

Mayer, R. E. & Moreno, R. (2003). Nine ways to reduce cognitive load in multimedia learning. *Educational Psychologist, 38*(1), 43-52.

Nelson, D.L., Reed, V.S., & Walling, J.R. (1976). Pictorial superiority effect. Journal of Experimental Psychology: Human Learning and Memory. 2(5), 523-528.

Paas, F. G. W. C, & Van Merriënboer, J. J. G. (1993). The efficiency of instructional conditions: An approach to combine mental effort and performance measures. *Human Factors: The Journal of the Human Factors and Ergonomics Society, 35*(4): 737–743.

Paivo, A. (1971). *Imagery and Verbal Processes.* New York: Holt, Rinehart & Winston.

Paivio, A. (1986). *Mental Representations: A Dual Coding Approach*. Oxford, UK: Oxford University.

Sweller, J. (2005). Implications of cognitive load theory for multimedia learning. In R. E. Mayer (Ed.), *The Cambridge Handbook of Multimedia Learning* (pp. 19-30). New York, NY: Cambridge University Press.

Sweller, J. (2008). Human cognitive architecture. In J. M. Spector, M. D. Merrill, J. V. Merriënboer, & M.P. Driscoll (Eds.), *Handbook of Research on Educational Communications and Technology 3rd ed.*, 369-381. New York, NY: Taylor & Francis Group.

Wastlund, E. (2007). Experimental Studies of Human-Computer Interaction: Working memory and mental workload in complex cognition. https://gupea.ub.gu.se/bitstream/2077/4693/1/gupea_2077_4693_1.pdf

Reading/Readability/Writing

S. Badgley. (February 20, 2015), Should your blog reading level be about 8th grade? Lantern.

Craig, J. & Scala, I. K. (2006). *Designing with Type: The Essential Guide to Typography, 5th ed*. Watson-Guptill. http://www.designingwithtype.com

Federal Plain Language Guidelines (2011) www.plainlanguage.gov/howto/guidelines/FederalPLGuidelines/index.cfm

Fleming, M., & Levie, W. H. (1993). *Principles from the Behavioral and Cognitive Sciences*. Englewood Cliffs, NJ: Educational Technology Publications.

Hartley, J. *Designing Instructional Text*. (1994). London: Kogan Page Ltd.

Kellogg, R.T., Whiteford, A.P., Turner, C.E., Cahill, M., & Mertens, A. (2013) Working memory in written composition: An evaluation of the 1996 model. *Journal of Writing Research*, 5(2), 159-190.

Kincaid J. P., Braby, R., & Mears J. (1988). Electronic authoring and delivery of technical information. *Journal of Instructional Development*. 11, 8–13.

Latham, J. S. (1991). The Effect of Outlines, Headings and Summaries on the Recall of Informational Text.

Lohr, L. (2003). *Creating Graphics for Learning and Performance*. Upper Saddle River, New Jersey: Pearson Education.

Mayer, R. E., Fennell, S., Farmer, L., & Campbell, J. (2004). A personalization effect in multimedia learning: Students learn better when words are in conversational style rather than formal style. Journal of Educational Psychology, 96 (2), 389-395.

McLaughlin, G., SMOG grading: A new readability formula. Journal of Reading, 1969. 12(8): p. 639-646.

Morkes, J. & Nielsen, J. (1998). Applying writing guidelines to Web pages.

Oppenheimer, D. (2005). Consequences of erudite vernacular utilized irrespective of necessity: Problems with using long words needlessly. *Applied Cognitive Psychology, 20*(2): 139–156. DOI: 10.1002/acp.1178.

Redish, J. G. (2007). *Letting Go of the Words: Writing Web Content That Works*. San Francisco, CA: Elsevier.

Redish, J. & Selzer, J. (1985) The place of readability formulas in technical communication. Technical Communication, 32 (4), 46-52.

Schriver, K. A. (1991, February). *Plain language for expert or lay audiences: Designing text using protocol-aided revision* (Technical Report No. 46). Center for the Study of Writing.

SMOG Calculator, ed:it Lab, The University of Nottingham.

Spyridakis, J.H. (2000). Guidelines for authoring comprehensible web pages and evaluating their success. Technical Communication, 47(3), 359-382.

Wright, P. (1980). The comprehension of tabulated information: Some similarities between reading prose and reading tables. National Society for Performance and Instruction Journal, 19(8), 25-29.

Usability, User Experience, Information Design

Costabile, M.F., De Marsico, M, Lanzilotti, R., Plantamura, V. L., & Roselli, T. (2005). On the usability evaluation of e-Learning applications. Proceedings of the 38th Annual Hawaii International Conference on System Sciences, 2005.

DeSalvo, K.B. (2010). Health literacy online: A guide for simplifying the user experience. The Office of Disease Prevention and Health Promotion, U.S. Department of Health and Human Services.

Dillon, A. (1992) Reading from paper versus screens: a critical review of the empirical literature. Ergonomics, 35(10), 1297-1326.

Gerhardt-Powals, J. (1996). Cognitive engineering principles for enhancing human-computer performance. International Journal of Human-Computer Interaction, 8(2), 189-211.

Jabr, F. (2013). The reading brain in the digital age: The science of paper versus screens. *Scientific American*.

Landesman, L. & Schroeder, W. (2000). Report 5: Organizing links. In Designing Information-Rich Web Sites. Bradford, MA: User Interface Engineering.

Molich, R., Ede, M. R., Kaasgaard, K., and Karyukin, B. (2004). Comparative usability evaluation. Behavior and Information Technology, 23(1).

Mukherjee, P., & Edmonds, G. S. (1994). Screen design: A review of research. In D. G. Beauchamp, R. A. Braden, & J. C. Baca (Eds.), Visual literacy in the digital age: Selected readings from the 25th annual conference of the International Visual Literacy Association, 112-118.

Myrberg, C. & Wiberg, N., (2015). Screen vs. paper: what is the difference for reading and learning? Insights. 28(2), 49–54.

Nielsen, J. (November 15, 2015). Legibility, readability, and comprehension: Making users read your words.

Nielsen, J. (April 17, 2009). F-shaped pattern for reading web content.

Nielsen, J. (May 6, 2008). How Little Do Users Read?

Spyridakis, J. H. (2000). Guidelines for authoring comprehensible web pages and evaluating their success. Technical Communication, 47(3), 359-282.

Usability.gov. Improving the user experience https://www.usability.gov

Usability Book of Knowledge http://www.usabilitybok.org/

U.S. Department of Health & Human Services. (2015). Glossary.

Web Accessibility in Mind (WebAIM) http://webaim.org

Index

Notes

About the Author

Patti Shank is an internationally recognized learning analyst, researcher, designer, and author who is cited as a leading international learning expert. She works with organizations to analyze and find solutions for organizational performance needs and is regularly asked to speak at conferences and train trainers, instructors, designers, and experts.

Patti has authored, co-authored, or edited numerous learning books and eBooks. She was an award-winning contributing editor for *Online Learning Magazine* and the research director for the eLearning Guild. You can find her articles and research in eLearning Guild publications, Magna Publications' *Online Classroom,* eLearning Industry, and ATD's *Science of Learning* and *Senior Leaders and Executives* blogs.

Patti lives in Colorado, USA, and loves to spend time with her fur babies and friends, and dance, walk, read, cook, and travel.

Printed in Great Britain
by Amazon

65544624R00098